M

DATE DUE

The Perfect S
Wedding

The Perfect Stranger's Guide to Wedding Ceremonies

A Guide to Etiquette in Other People's Religious Ceremonies

Edited by Stuart M. Matlins

Walking Together, Finding the Way

SKYLIGHT PATHS Publishing
WOODSTOCK, VERMONT

The Perfect Stranger's Guide to Wedding Ceremonies:
A Guide to Etiquette in Other People's Religious Ceremonies

© 2000 by SkyLight Paths Publishing

SkyLight Paths and colophon are trademarks of LongHill Partners, Inc. registered in the U.S. Patent and Trademark Office.

Library of Congress Cataloging-in-Publication Data
The perfect stranger's guide to wedding ceremonies : a guide to etiquette in other people's religious ceremonies / edited by Stuart M. Matlins.
        p. cm.
ISBN 1-893361-19-5 (pbk.)
1. Wedding etiquette. 2. Religious etiquette—United States. 3. United States—Religion—20th century. I. Matlins, Stuart M.
BJ2051 .P45 2000
395.2'2—dc21
                        00-059575

10 9 8 7 6 5 4 3 2 1

Manufactured in the United States of America
Cover design by Drena Fagen
Text design by Chelsea Dippel

Published by SkyLight Paths Publishing
A Division of LongHill Partners, Inc.
Sunset Farm Offices, Route 4, P.O. Box 237
Woodstock, VT 05091
Tel: (802) 457-4000   Fax: (802) 457-4004
www.skylightpaths.com

Contents

Acknowledgments

A book such as this is the product of many contributions by many people. It could be no other way given the broad tapestry of religions in North America. This book, with its focus on etiquette at wedding ceremonies, is based on the two award-winning volumes of *How to Be a Perfect Stranger: A Guide to Etiquette in Other People's Religious Ceremonies.*

Instrumental in the evolution of *How to Be a Perfect Stranger* were Richard A. Siegel and William Shanken, who developed the original concept and helped get the first volume into gear. Stuart M. Matlins, publisher of SkyLight Paths, developed the methodology for obtaining the information, and with Arthur J. Magida, editorial director of SkyLight Paths, oversaw the research and writing and provided the impetus for the project. Sandra Korinchak, editor, shepherded the project from start to finish with the help of Jennifer Goneau, editorial assistant. Research assistant Susan Parks helped ensure that certain denominations responded promptly to our requests. And Jordan D. Wood generously assumed an initiative that delighted us all. Michael Schwartzentruber, series editor of Northstone Publishing, compiled the Canadian data.

The Native American/First Nations information was provided by Dan Wildcat, a member of the Wyuchi Tribe of Oklahoma and a sociology professor at the Haskell Indian Nations University in Lawrence, Kansas.

All other chapters were based on information obtained from an extensive questionnaire filled out by clergy and other religious experts coast-to-coast. Without the help of the following, this book would never have become a reality:

Timothy Addington, Executive Director of Ministry Advancement, The Evangelical Free Church of North America, Minneapolis, Minnesota

Rev. E. Wayne Antworth, Director of Stewardship and Communications, The Reformed Church in America, New York, New York

Dr. Satyendra Banerjee, priest and past-president, Bengali Cultural Society of British Columbia

Leroy Beachy, Beachy Amish Mennonite, Millersburg, Ohio

Ronald R. Brannon, General Secretary,
The Wesleyan Church, Indianapolis, Indiana

Rabbi Gary M. Bretton-Granatoor, Director of Interreligious Affairs,
Union of American Hebrew Congregations (Reform),
New York, New York

Ellen K. Campbell, Executive Director,
Canadian Unitarian Council, Toronto, Ontario

Marj Carpenter, former Mission Interpreter,
Presbyterian Church (USA), Louisville, Kentucky

Sharon Glidden Cole, Administrative Assistant,
Executive Offices, The Christian and Missionary Alliance,
Colorado Springs, Colorado

Glenn Cooper, former Director of Communications,
The Presbyterian Church in Canada, Pictou, Nova Scotia

Archpriest George Corey, Vicar,
Antiochian Orthodox Archdiocese, New York, New York

Scott Dickson, Public Affairs (Canada), Jehovah's Witnesses,
Watch Tower Bible and Tract Society of Canada

Alf Dumont (member, First Nations),
St. John's United Church, Alliston, Ontario

Rev. Ora W. Eads, General Superintendent,
The Christian Congregation, Inc., LaFollette, Tennessee

Rabbi Moshe Edelman, Associate Director of Regions and
Director of Leadership Development,
United Synagogue of Conservative Judaism, New York, New York

Eugene J. Fisher, Associate Director of the Secretariat for
Ecumenical and Interreligious Affairs of the National Conference
of Catholic Bishops, Washington, D.C.

Ted George, Librarian, Greek Orthodox Cathedral of the Annunciation,
Baltimore, Maryland

Rev. Lance Gifford, Rector, St. John's Episcopal Church,
Baltimore, Maryland

James S. Golding, Editor, *The [Greek] Orthodox Observer,*
New York, New York

Steven D. Goodman, Professor of Indian and Tibetan Buddhism,
Institute of Buddhist Studies, Berkeley, California

Lois Hammond, Evangelical Free Church of Canada,
Langley, British Columbia

Father Gregory Havrilak, Director of Communications,
Orthodox Church in North America, New York, New York

Marvin Hein, General Secretary,
The General Conference of Mennonite Brethren, Fresno, California

Hoyt Hickman, now retired from the General Board of Discipleship,
United Methodist Church, Nashville, Tennessee

Rev. Donald E. Hodgins, Central Canada District,
The Wesleyan Church of Canada, Belleville, Ontario

Hans Holznagel, Public Relations Manager,
United Church of Christ, Cleveland, Ohio

Ibrahim Hooper, Council on American-Islamic Relations,
Washington, D.C.

Bede Hubbard, Assistant General Secretary,
Canadian Conference of Catholic Bishops, Ottawa, Ontario

John Hurley, Archivist and Public Relations Officer,
Unitarian Universalist Association of Congregations,
Boston, Massachusetts

Ralph Janes, Communications Director,
Seventh-day Adventist Church in Canada

Rev. B. Edgar Johnson, Former General Secretary,
The Church of the Nazarene, Kansas City, Missouri

Wesley Johnson, Executive Assistant,
The Evangelical Free Church of North America, Minneapolis, Minnesota

Hari Dharam Kaur Khalsa, The Mukhia Sardarni Sahiba,
Sikh Dharma of New Mexico, Española, New Mexico

Rev. Dr. Ralph Lebold, Past President Conrad Grebel College,
University of Waterloo, Waterloo, Ontario

Don LeFevre, Manager of Public Affairs Department,
The Church of Jesus Christ of Latter-day Saints, Salt Lake City, Utah

David A. Linscheid, Communications Director,
General Conference Mennonite Church, Newton, Kansas

Barbara Liotscos, Consultant for Ministry and Worship,
The Anglican Church of Canada, Toronto, Ontario

Stan Litke, Executive Director,
Christian Church (Disciples of Christ) in Canada, Calgary, Alberta

Dr. Gordon MacDonald, Pentecostal Holiness Church of Canada,
Surrey, British Columbia

Rev. David Mahsman, Director of News and Information,
The Lutheran Church–Missouri Synod, St. Louis, Missouri

Mike McDonald, Pulpit Minister, The Church of Christ, Monahans, Texas

The Very Reverend Protopresbyter Frank P. Miloro,
The American Carpatho-Russian Orthodox Greek Catholic
Diocese of the U.S.A., Johnstown, Pennsylvania

Ronald R. Minor, General Secretary,
The Pentecostal Church of God, Joplin, Missouri

Dana Mullen, Clerk–Representative Meeting,
Canadian Yearly Meeting, Ottawa, Ontario

Dr. Paul Nelson, Director for Worship,
Evangelical Lutheran Church in America, Chicago, Illinois

Father Louis Noplos, Assistant Pastor,
Greek Orthodox Cathedral of the Annunciation, Baltimore, Maryland

Rev. Dr. David Ocea, The Romanian Orthodox
Episcopate of North America, Grass Lake, Minnesota

Sara Palmer, Program Secretary, The Wider Quaker Fellowship,
Philadelphia, Pennsylvania

Mark Parent, Ph.D., Pereaux United Baptist Church,
Pereaux, Nova Scotia

Richard Payne, Dean, Institute of Buddhist Studies,
Berkeley, California

Wardell Payne, Research Consultant on African American
Religions, Washington, D.C.

Laurie Peach, Staff Writer,
The First Church of Christ, Scientist, Boston, Massachusetts

Pal S. Purewal, former president,
Sikh Society of Alberta, Edmonton, Alberta

Rev. Frank Reid, Senior Pastor,
Bethel African Methodist Episcopal Church, Baltimore, Maryland

Dr. George W. Reid, Director of the Biblical Research Institute,
Seventh-day Adventists, Silver Spring, Maryland

Raymond Richardson, Writing Department,
Jehovah's Witnesses, Brooklyn, New York

Rev. John Roberts, Pastor,
Woodbrook Baptist Church, Baltimore, Maryland

Michael R. Rothaar, Acting Director for Worship,
Evangelical Lutheran Church in America, Chicago, Illinois

Howard E. Royer, Director of Interpretation,
The Church of the Brethren, Elgin, Indiana

John Schlenck, Librarian and Music Director,
Vedanta Society of New York, New York

Bhante Seelawimala, Professor of Theravada Buddhism,
Institute of Buddhist Studies, Berkeley, California

Bruce Smith, Public Affairs,
The Church of Jesus Christ of Latter-day Saints, North York, Ontario

Rabbi David Sulomm Stein, Beit Tikvah Congregation
(Reconstructionist), Baltimore, Maryland

Dr. Suwanda Sugunasiri, President, Buddhist Council of Canada;
Teaching Staff and Research Associate in Buddhist Studies,
Trinity College, University of Toronto

Trish Swanson, Former Director, Office of Public Information, Baha'is of
the United States, New York, New York

James Taylor, United Church of Canada,
co-founder Wood Lake Books Inc., Okanagan Centre, British Columbia

Imam Michael Abdur Rashid Taylor,
Islamic Chaplaincy Services Canada, Bancroft, Ontario

Dr. David A. Teutsch, President,
Reconstructionist Rabbinical College, Wyncote, Pennsylvania

Juleen Turnage, Secretary of Public Relations,
Assemblies of God, Springfield, Missouri

Jerry Van Marter, Mission Interpreter and International News,
Presbyterian Church (USA), Louisville, Kentucky

Lois Volstad, Executive Secretary, Executive Offices,
The Christian and Missionary Alliance, Colorado Springs, Colorado

Rev. Kenn Ward, editor of *Canada Lutheran*, Winnipeg, Manitoba

Deborah Weiner, Director, Public Relations,
Unitarian Universalist Association of Congregations, Boston, Massachusetts

Rabbi Tzvi Hersh Weinreb, Shomrei Emunah Congregation
(Orthodox), Baltimore, Maryland

M. Victor Westberg, Manager, Committees on Publications,
The First Church of Christ, Scientist, Boston, Massachusetts

Ronald D. Williams, Communications Officer,
International Church of the Foursquare Gospel, Los Angeles, California

Clifford L. Willis, Director of News and Information,
The Christian Church (Disciples of Christ), Indianapolis, Indiana

Pamela Zivari, Director, Office of Public Information,
Baha'is of the United States, New York, New York

Introduction

A marriage is a joyous event—that can be made awkward if you're unfamiliar with the religious tradition in which the wedding takes place and end up uncertain about how to behave.

It is no longer uncommon to be invited to the wedding of a relative or friend of a different faith from one's own; and such exposure to the religious ways of others can give us a deep appreciation for the extraordinary diversity of faith and the variety of ways it surfaces.

Yet, in spite of the joy of the celebration, we may be uncomfortable or uncertain: What do I do? Or wear? Or say? What should I *avoid* doing, wearing, saying? What will happen during the ceremony? How long will it last? What does each ritual mean? What are the basic beliefs of this particular religion?

These are just some of the practical questions that arise because of the fundamental foreignness of the experience. *The Perfect Stranger's Guide to Wedding Ceremonies* addresses these concerns in a straightforward and non-judgmental manner. Its goal is to make a well-meaning guest feel comfortable, participate to the fullest extent feasible, and avoid violating anyone's religious principles. It is not intended to be a comprehensive primer on theology. It's a guidebook to a land where we may be strangers, but where, on the whole, those on whose celebratory turf we soon will be treading want us to be as comfortable, relaxed and unperturbed as possible. There is nothing more indicative of friendship than to welcome "the stranger"—and for "the stranger" to do his or her homework before entering an unfamiliar house of worship or religious ceremony.

We've all been strangers at one time or another or in one place or another. If this book helps turn the "strange" into the less "exotic" and into the less confusing (but not into the ordinary), then it will have satisfied its goal of minimizing our anxiety and our confusion when face-to-face with another faith—while, at the same time, deepening our appreciation and our understanding of that faith. While we pray and worship in thousands of churches, synagogues, mosques and temples around the country, these denominational fences are not insurmountable. Indeed, these fences come complete with gates. It is often up to us to find the key to those gates. We hope that this book helps in the search for that key.

A few notes on the way in which *The Perfect Stranger's Guide to Wedding Ceremonies* was compiled and structured:

Each chapter is devoted to a particular religion or denomination. Basic research was conducted through an extensive questionnaire that was completed in almost all cases by the national office of each religion and denomination. For those denominations whose national office did not respond to the questionnaire, we obtained responses from clergy of that particular faith. To minimize error in nuance, drafts of the entry for each chapter were forwarded for comments to those who had filled out the questionnaire.

The Perfect Stranger's Guide to Wedding Ceremonies is not intended as a substitute for the social common sense that should prevail at social or religious events. For example, if a chapter advises readers that guests may use a flash or a video camera, the equipment should not be used in such a way that it disrupts the religious ceremony or disturbs participants in the ceremony or other guests.

The guidelines in this book are just that. They should not be mistaken for firm and unbendable rules. Religious customs, traditions and rituals for weddings are strongly influenced by where people live and the part of the world from which their ancestors originated. As a result, there may be a variety of practices within a single denomination. This book is a general guide to wedding ceremonies, and it's important to remember that *particulars* may sometimes vary broadly within individual denominations.

Terms within each chapter are those used by that religion. For example, the terms "New Testament" and "Old Testament" appear in several chapters about various Christian denominations. Some Jewish people may find this disconcerting since they recognize only one testament. The purpose is not to offend, but to portray these religions as they portray themselves. The goal of this book, one must remember, is to enable us to be "a perfect stranger." And "perfection" might well begin with recognizing that when we join others in celebrating events in their religion's vernacular, we are obliged, as guests, to know the customs, rituals and language of the event.

For future editions of *The Perfect Stranger's Guide to Wedding Ceremonies*, we encourage readers to write to us and suggest ways in which this book could be made more useful to them and to others. Are there additional subjects that future editions should cover? Have important subtleties been missed? We see this book—and the evolution of our unique North American society—as an ongoing work-in-progress, and we welcome your comments. Please write to:

Editors, *The Perfect Stranger's Guide to Wedding Ceremonies*
SkyLight Paths Publishing
Sunset Farm Offices, Rte. 4
P.O. Box 237
Woodstock, Vermont 05091

1

African American Methodist Churches

(known as the African Methodist Episcopal Church; the African Methodist Episcopal Zion Church; the Christian Methodist Episcopal Church; the Union American Methodist Episcopal Church, Inc.; and the African Union First Colored Methodist Protestant Church)

HISTORY AND BELIEFS

The African American Methodist churches began in the late 18th century and throughout the 19th century as a reaction to racial discrimination. The broader Methodist Church had originated in the early 18th century in England under the preaching of John Wesley, an Anglican priest who was a prodigious evangelical preacher, writer and organizer. While a student at Oxford University, he and his brother had led the Holy Club of devout students, whom scoffers called the "Methodists."

Wesley's teachings affirmed the freedom of human will as promoted by grace. He saw each person's depth of sin matched by the height of sanctification to which the Holy Spirit, the empowering spirit of God, can lead persons of faith.

Although Wesley remained an Anglican and disavowed attempts to form a new church, Methodism eventually became another church body. During a conference in Baltimore, Maryland, in 1784, the Methodist Church was founded as an ecclesiastical organization and the first Methodist bishop in the United States was elected.

Blacks had originally been attracted to the Methodist Church because its original evangelism made no distinctions between the races, and John

19

Wesley, the founder of Methodism, had strongly denounced slavery and the African slave trade on the grounds that they were contrary to the will of God. Initially, many Methodists—clergy and laity—opposed slavery, called upon church members to desist from trafficking in slaves, and urged them to free any slaves they did own. But as Methodists became more numerous in the South, the Church gradually muted its opposition to slavery.

In 1787, black members of Philadelphia's St. George's Methodist Episcopal Church withdrew from the church after experiencing discrimination, and the African Methodist Episcopal Church was officially established as a denomination on April 16, 1816.

The African Methodist Episcopal Zion Church was founded in 1796 after blacks were denied the sacraments and full participation in the John Street Methodist Church in New York City, located in a state with the largest slave population outside of the South.

And the Christian Methodist Episcopal Church was founded in 1870, four years after African American members of the Methodist Episcopal Church, South (M.E.C.S.) petitioned the Church to be allowed to create a separate Church that would be governed by the M.E.C.S. In 1870, the General Conference of the M.E.C.S. voted to let black members be constituted as an independent church, not as a subordinate body. This reflected the post–Civil War period's imperatives calling for independence for African Americans and the reconstruction of American society.

Two smaller African American Methodist churches are the Union American Methodist Episcopal Church, Inc., with 15,000 members in 55 congregations, and the African Union First Colored Methodist Protestant Church, with 5,000 members in 33 congregations. Both of these were founded in 1865.

Local African American Methodist churches are called "charges." Their ministers are appointed by the bishop at an annual conference, and each church elects its own administrative board, which initiates planning and sets local goals and policies.

Number of U.S. churches:
African Methodist Episcopal: 8,000
African Methodist Episcopal Zion: 3,100
African Union First Colored Methodist Protestant Church: 33
Christian Methodist Episcopal Church: 2,300
Union American Methodist Episcopal Church, Inc.: 55

Number of U. S. members:
African Methodist Episcopal: 3.5 million
African Methodist Episcopal Zion: 1.2 million
African Union First Colored Methodist Protestant Church: 5,000
Christian Methodist Episcopal Church: 718,900
Union American Methodist Episcopal Church, Inc.: 15,000
(*data from the* Directory of American Religious Bodies *and the*
1998 Yearbook of American and Canadian Churches)

MARRIAGE CEREMONY

African American Methodist denominations affirm that marriage is the uniting of a man and a woman in a union which is intended—and which is pledged—to be lifelong.

The marriage ceremony is a service in itself. It may last between 15 and 30 minutes.

BEFORE THE CEREMONY

Are guests usually invited by a formal invitation?
Yes.

If not stated explicitly, should one assume that children are invited?
No.

If one can't attend, what should one do?
RSVP with your regrets and send a gift.

APPROPRIATE ATTIRE

Men: A jacket and tie. No head covering is required.

Women: A dress. The arms do not necessarily have to be covered nor do hems have to be below the knees. Open-toed shoes and modest jewelry are permissible. No head covering is required.

There are no rules regarding colors of clothing.

GIFTS

Is a gift customarily expected?
Yes. Such gifts as small appliances, sheets, towels or other household gifts are appropriate.

Should gifts be brought to the ceremony?
No, send them to the home of the newlyweds.

THE CEREMONY

Where will the ceremony take place?

Usually in the main sanctuary of a church.

When should guests arrive and where should they sit?

Arrive early. Depending on the setting, ushers may show guests where to sit.

If arriving late, are there times when a guest should *not* enter the ceremony?

Ushers will usually assist latecomers.

Are there times when a guest should *not* leave the ceremony?

No.

Who are the major officiants, leaders or participants at the ceremony and what do they do?

- *The pastor,* who officiates.
- *The bride and groom and their wedding party.*

What books are used?

Books vary from congregation to congregation within each of the African American Methodist denominations, but the Bibles usually used are the King James Version, the New Revised Standard or the New International Version. Also, most African Methodist Episcopal churches use *The AMEC Bicentennial Hymnal* (Nashville, Tenn.: The African Methodist Episcopal Church, 1984); African Methodist Episcopal Zion churches use *The Songs of Zion* (Nashville, Tenn.: Abingdon Press, 1982); and Christian Methodist Episcopal churches use *The Hymnal of the Christian Methodist Episcopal Church* (Memphis, Tenn.: The CME Publishing House, 1987).

To indicate the order of the ceremony:

A program will be provided.

Will a guest who is not a member of an African American Methodist denomination be expected to do anything other than sit?

Standing and kneeling with the congregation, reading prayers aloud, and singing with congregants are all optional. Guests are welcome to participate if this does not compromise their personal beliefs. If guests do not wish to kneel or stand, they may remain seated at these times.

Are there any parts of the ceremony in which a guest who is not a member of an African American Methodist denomination should *not* participate?

Yes. Holy Communion may be offered at the service. Methodists invite all to receive Holy Communion, but guests should be aware that partaking of communion is regarded as an act of identification with Christianity. Feel free to remain seated as others go forward for communion. Likewise, if communion bread and cups are passed among the pews, feel free to pass them along without partaking.

If not disruptive to the service, is it okay to:

- **Take pictures?** Possibly. Ask ushers.
- **Use a video camera?** Possibly. Ask ushers.
- **Use a flash camera?** Possibly. Ask ushers.
- **Use a tape recorder?** Possibly. Ask ushers.

Will contributions to the church be collected at the ceremony?

No.

AFTER THE CEREMONY

Is there usually a reception after the ceremony?

There is often a reception that may last one to two hours. It may be at a home, a catering facility or in the same building as the ceremony. Ordinarily, food and beverages are served and there is dancing and music. Alcoholic beverages may be served.

Would it be considered impolite to neither eat nor drink?

No.

Is there a grace or benediction before eating or drinking?

No.

Is there a grace or benediction after eating or drinking?

No.

Is there a traditional greeting for the family?

No. Just offer your congratulations.

Is there a traditional form of address for clergy who may be at the reception?

"Reverend" or "Pastor."

Is it okay to leave early?

Yes, but usually only after toasts have been made and the wedding cake has been served.

2

Assemblies of God

HISTORY AND BELIEFS

In 1914, when the Assemblies of God were formed, America had, for several years, been in the midst of a major revival movement. Many involved spontaneously spoke "in tongues" (or in a language unknown to those speaking it) and claims were made of divine healing that saved lives. Since many of these experiences were associated with the coming of the Holy Spirit (the empowering quality of God) on the Day of Pentecost, participants in the revival were called Pentecostals.

After mainline churches divorced themselves from the revival phenomenon, about 300 Pentecostal leaders met in Hot Springs, Arkansas. After three days of prayer, they decided to organize themselves not as a new denomination, but as a loose-knit fellowship called the General Council of the Assemblies of God. Two years later, the Council realized the need to establish standards of doctrinal truths.

In part, this Statement of Fundamental Truths asserts that the Bible is divinely inspired and is infallible; the one true God created earth and heaven, redeems humanity from its sins and consists of the Father, the Son (Jesus Christ) and the Holy Spirit; Jesus has always existed and is without beginning or end; humanity was created good and upright, but, by falling into sin, incurred physical and spiritual death; humanity's only hope for salvation from sin and spiritual death is through Christ.

The Assemblies of God is one of the more quickly growing churches in the United States: Since 1960, membership has grown from around 500,000 to more than 1.4 million. The Church is especially keen on using conversion to swell its ranks. In the last decade, the largest number of conversions—61,272—has been in the Church's southwest region

(California, Nevada, Arizona and Colorado). Many of these new members are Hispanic-speaking.

U.S. churches: 12,000
U.S. membership: 1.4 million
(1998 data from the Assemblies of God)

MARRIAGE CEREMONY

The Assemblies of God teaches that the family was the first institution ordained by God in the Garden of Eden. The basis for a family is marriage between two consenting adults. Marriage, which is not to be entered into lightly, is said to be "until death do us part."

The marriage ceremony is a ceremony in itself and may last 30 to 60 minutes.

BEFORE THE CEREMONY

Are guests usually invited by a formal invitation?
Yes.

If not stated explicitly, should one assume that children are invited?
No.

If one can't attend, what should one do?
RSVP by card or letter with regrets.

APPROPRIATE ATTIRE

Men: A jacket and tie. No head covering is required.

Women: A dress. Clothing need not cover the arms and hems need not reach below the knees. Open-toed shoes and modest jewelry are permissible. No head covering is required.

There are no rules regarding colors of clothing.

GIFTS

Is a gift customarily expected?
Yes. Cash, bonds, or small household items are most frequently given.

Should gifts be brought to the ceremony?
Yes.

THE CEREMONY

Where will the ceremony take place?

In the main sanctuary of the church.

When should guests arrive and where should they sit?

Arrive shortly before the time for which the ceremony has been called. Ushers will usually advise guests about where to sit.

If arriving late, are there times when a guest should *not* enter the ceremony?

Do not enter during the processional or recessional of the wedding party.

Are there times when a guest should *not* leave the ceremony?

No.

Who are the major officiants, leaders or participants at the ceremony and what do they do?

◗ *The pastor,* who officiates.
◗ *The bride and groom and their wedding party.*

What books are used?

Ordinarily, the pastor uses various wedding ceremonies chosen by the bride and groom. These include references to and passages from the Scriptures.

To indicate the order of the ceremony:

A program will be distributed.

Will a guest who is not a member of the Assemblies of God be expected to do anything other than sit?

Guests of other faiths are expected to stand when other guests rise during the ceremony. It is optional for them to kneel and to sing with the congregants and to join them in reading prayers aloud.

Are there any parts of the ceremony in which a guest who is not a member of the Assemblies of God should *not* participate?

No.

If not disruptive to the ceremony, is it okay to:

◗ **Take pictures?** Possibly.
◗ **Use a flash?** Possibly.
◗ **Use a video camera?** Possibly.
◗ **Use a tape recorder?** Possibly.

(Note: Policies regarding still and video cameras and tape recorders vary with each church. Check with the local pastor before using such equipment during a service.)

Will contributions to the church be collected at the ceremony?
No.

AFTER THE CEREMONY

Is there usually a reception after the ceremony?
Yes. It may be in the same building where the wedding ceremony was held or in a catering hall. Receptions vary from full-course meals to a stand-up reception at which cake, mints, nuts and punch are served. There will be no alcoholic beverages. The reception may last 30 to 60 minutes.

Would it be considered impolite to neither eat nor drink?
No.

Is there a grace or benediction before eating or drinking?
No.

Is there a grace or benediction after eating or drinking?
No.

Is there a traditional greeting for the family?
Just offer your congratulations.

Is there a traditional form of address for clergy who may be at the reception?
Either "Pastor" or "Reverend."

Is it okay to leave early?
Yes, unless it is a formal meal.

3
Baha'i

HISTORY AND BELIEFS

The Baha'i religion sprang out of an Islamic movement known as the Babi faith, which was founded in the mid-19th century in Persia (now southern Iran) by Mirza Ali Muhammad, a direct descendant of the Prophet Muhammad. By proclaiming himself to be the Bab, which literally means "gate" or "door," Ali Muhammad announced that he was the forerunner of the Universal Messenger of God, who would usher in an era of justice and peace.

In 1850, the Bab was killed by a firing squad in Tabriz, Persia, upon the order of the grand vizier of the new Shah of Iran. The grand vizier was acting on behalf of traditional Islamic clergy in his country, who were alarmed at what they perceived to be the heretical doctrine being taught by the Bab and also by the fact that he was gaining followers.

In 1863, one of the Bab's 18 original closest disciples, Baha'u'llah, declared, while he was in exile in Iraq, that he was "He Whom God Shall Manifest," the messianic figure whom the Bab had predicted. He was soon banished by the Iraqi government to Istanbul and then to Adrianapole, where he stayed for five years.

Agitation from opponents caused the Turkish government to send the exiles to Acre, Palestine, where Baha'u'llah spent his last years. Upon his death, his eldest son, Abdu'l-Baha, "The Servant of Baha," led the faith, as had been determined in his father's will. With his death in 1921, leadership fell, as stipulated in Abdu'l-Baha's will, to his eldest grandson, Shoghi Effendi, "The Guardian of the Cause of God," who devoted himself to expanding the worldwide Baha'i community, establishing its central administrative offices in Haifa, and translating the writings of his great-grandfather, Baha'u'llah.

Central to Baha'i beliefs is the unity of all religions and of all humanity. God, Baha'is teach, may be unknowable, but the divine presence manifests itself in various ways. Among these are the creation of the world and the prophets, beginning with Adam, and continuing through the Jewish prophets, Buddha, Krishna, Zoroaster, Jesus and Muhammad, who was succeeded by Baha'u'llah. Each prophet represents a divine message which was appropriate for the era in which he appeared. Baha'is believe that other prophets may come in the future, and that there is no last revelation or final prophet.

Members are elected to Baha'i's approximately 20,000 local spiritual councils, of which there are about 1,700 in the United States, and 324 in Canada. Members are also elected to 174 national spiritual assemblies throughout the world. These culminate in a Universal House of Justice, which has administrative, judicial and legislative functions and the authority to frame new rules for situations not provided for in the writings of Baha'u'llah.

There are now more than five million Baha'is in 233 countries and territories. Throughout the world, the Baha'i faith has only seven houses of worship, one on each continent. The house of worship in North America is in Wilmette, Illinois. Locally, Baha'is may meet for worship or for communal activities in homes or Baha'i centers. The minimum number of Baha'is that can comprise a local community is two, but nine are required for a local spiritual council.

U.S. communities: 7,000
U.S. membership: 130,000
(data from the Office of Public Information, Baha'is of the United States)

MARRIAGE CEREMONY

The Baha'i faith teaches that the family is the basic unit of society and that monogamous marriage is the foundation of family life. Also, preparation for marriage is essential for ensuring a happy marriage. Preparation includes parental approval for the choice of a spouse. This does not mean that Baha'i marriages are arranged since Baha'is marry the person of their choice. But once the choice is made, parents have the right and the obligation to weigh carefully whether to give their consent and, thus, to guide their offspring in one of life's most important decisions.

Baha'is encourage interracial marriages since these stress humanity's essential oneness. The faith also does not discourage interfaith marriages.

The Baha'i faith allows divorce, although it strongly discourages it. If a Baha'i couple decides to seek a divorce, they must live apart from each other for at least one year—the "year of patience"—while they attempt to reconcile. If they still desire a divorce after those 12 months, it is granted.

The Baha'i faith does not have a standard wedding service. Its only stipulation for a wedding is that the bride and groom must exchange vows in front of two witnesses designated by the local Baha'i spiritual council. The vow repeated by the bride and groom is, "We will all verily abide by the Will of God." For a Baha'i, that Will implies all of the commitments associated with marriage, including to love, honor and cherish; to care for each other, regardless of health or wealth; and to share with and serve each other.

Other than meeting the criteria regarding witnesses and the bride and groom reciting the vows, a Baha'i wedding may be as simple or elaborate as a couple wishes.

The length of the wedding varies, depending on its content.

BEFORE THE CEREMONY

Are guests usually invited by a formal invitation?

Either by a written invitation or a telephone call.

If not stated explicitly, should one assume that children are invited?

Yes.

If one can't attend, what should one do?

Depending on one's personal preference, one may send flowers or a gift to the couple along with writing or telephoning your regrets that you cannot attend.

APPROPRIATE ATTIRE

Men: A jacket and tie. No head covering is required.

Women: A dress. Clothing need not cover the arms or reach below the knees. No head covering is required. Women may wear open-toed shoes and/or modest jewelry.

There are no rules regarding colors of clothing.

GIFTS

Is a gift customarily expected?

Yes. Appropriate gifts are whatever is the norm in one's culture.

Should gifts be brought to the ceremony?

They may be brought to the ceremony or the reception or sent to the home of the newlyweds.

THE CEREMONY

Where will the ceremony take place?

Baha'i weddings may be held wherever the bride and groom desire.

When should guests arrive and where should they sit?

Arrive at the time for which the service has been called. At some weddings, there may be ushers to advise guests on where to sit.

If arriving late, are there times when a guest should *not* enter the ceremony?

No.

Are there times when a guest should *not* leave the ceremony?

No.

Who are the major officiants, leaders or participants at the ceremony and what do they do?

◪ *The bride, the groom and two witnesses approved by the local spiritual council and who need not be Baha'is.*

What books are used?

There are no standard readings at Baha'i weddings. Whatever is read is chosen by the bride and groom and usually includes writings from Baha'i and other faiths, and other poetry and prose.

To indicate the order of the ceremony:

There may be a program or periodic announcements.

Will a guest who is not a Baha'i be expected to do anything other than sit?

No.

Are there any parts of the ceremony in which a guest who is not a Baha'i should *not* participate?

No.

If not disruptive to the ceremony, is it okay to:

- **Take pictures?** Yes.
- **Use a flash?** Yes.
- **Use a video camera?** Yes.
- **Use a tape recorder?** Yes.

Will contributions to the house of worship be collected at the ceremony?

No.

AFTER THE CEREMONY

Is there usually a reception after the ceremony?

Possibly, depending on personal preference. If there is a reception, there will probably be food, but no alcoholic beverages, since members of the Baha'i faith do not drink alcohol. There may also be music and dancing at the reception.

Would it be considered impolite to neither eat nor drink?

No.

Is there a grace or benediction before eating or drinking?

No.

Is there a grace or benediction after eating or drinking?

No.

Is there a traditional greeting for the family?

No.

Is there a traditional form of address for clergy who may be at the reception?

No, since there are no clergy in the Baha'i faith.

Is it okay to leave early?

Yes.

4

Baptist

HISTORY AND BELIEFS

The Baptist churches descend from the spiritual ferment generated by 17th century English Puritanism. Essentially, Baptists believe in the authority of the Bible, the right to privately interpret it, baptizing only those old enough to profess belief for themselves and strict separation of church and state.

Although there are about two dozen different branches and divisions of Baptist churches in the United States, there are essentially two separate schools of the faith: The General and the Particular. General Baptists believe in a universal atonement in which Christ died for all; Particular Baptists believe in the limited or "particular" death of Christ for believers only.

The movement began in England in the early 17th century. Its founder, John Smyth, moved to Holland in 1607 seeking religious liberty. Some early founders of Massachusetts, including the first president of Harvard, held Baptist beliefs. Although the first Baptist church in the colonies was founded in Providence, Rhode Island, in 1639, Philadelphia became the center of Baptist life during the colonial era.

In 1845, the white Baptist churches had separated into a northern and a southern group, with the northern division opposed to the extension of slavery. After the Civil War, the number of Black churches increased swiftly, mostly because Baptist principles appealed to Blacks and also because the autonomy allowed in individual churches meant that Black Baptist churches could operate without interference from white society. Canadian Baptists did not suffer from racial disunity but from theological disunity arising out of the Fundamentalist-Modernist controversy of the 1920s.

Today, the two largest Baptist denominations are the Southern Baptist Convention and the National Baptist Convention, U.S.A. Inc. The former has more than 15 million members and its founding in 1845 centered around a missionary impulse. The latter, with about 8 million members, is the largest African-American religious association in the United States.

In Canada, three Baptist groups are significant: The Federation Baptists, divided into four conventions; The Fellowship Baptists; and the North American Baptists (German descent).

U.S. churches: 91,000
U.S. membership: 34 million
(*data from the* 1998 Yearbook of American and Canadian Churches)

Canadian churches: 3,137
Canadian membership: 363,251
(*data from the* 1998 Yearbook of American and Canadian Churches)

MARRIAGE CEREMONY

Baptist denominations affirm that marriage is considered to be a three-way covenant between a woman, a man and God, who is represented at the marriage ceremony by the pastor, the congregation and the Holy Spirit (the empowering spirit of God).

The ceremony takes about 30 to 60 minutes and is a ceremony in itself.

BEFORE THE CEREMONY

Are guests usually invited by a formal invitation?
Yes.

If not stated explicitly, should one assume that children are invited?
No.

If one can't attend, what should one do?
RSVP with regrets and send a gift.

APPROPRIATE ATTIRE

Men: A suit or a jacket and tie. No head covering is required.

Women: A dress. Clothing should cover the arms and hems should reach below the knees. Open-toed shoes and modest jewelry allowed. No head covering is required.

There are no rules regarding colors of clothing.

GIFTS

Is a gift customarily expected?

Yes. Often appropriate are such household items as sheets, kitchenware or small household appliances.

Should gifts be brought to the ceremony?

Send gifts to the home of the newlyweds.

THE CEREMONY

Where will the ceremony take place?

Either in a church or a home.

When should guests arrive and where should they sit?

Arrive about 10 minutes before the time for which the ceremony has been called. Ushers will advise guests where to sit.

If arriving late, are there times when a guest should *not* enter the ceremony?

Do not enter during the procession or recession of the wedding party.

Are there times when a guest should *not* leave the ceremony?

Do not leave before the ceremony has ended.

Who are the major officiants, leaders or participants at the ceremony and what do they do?

- *The pastor*, who performs the ceremony.
- *The bride and groom.*
- *Musicians*, who provide music before, during and after the ceremony.

What books are used?

Only the pastor uses a text, which is invariably the Bible. Several translations of the Bible may be used, especially the King James Version, the New International Version and the New Revised Standard Version. All are distributed by several publishers. Many Canadian Baptist churches use *The Hymnal* (Brantford, ON: Baptist Federation of Canada, 1973).

To indicate the order of the ceremony:

No such guidance is needed for those present since the ceremony is relatively brief and there is no participation by guests.

Will a guest who is not a Baptist be expected to do anything other than sit?

No.

Are there any parts of the ceremony in which a guest who is not a Baptist should *not* participate?
No.

If not disruptive to the ceremony, is it okay to:
▪ **Take pictures?** Yes, but only with prior permission of the pastor.
▪ **Use a flash?** Yes, but only with prior permission of the pastor.
▪ **Use a video camera?** Yes, but only with prior permission of the pastor.
▪ **Use a tape recorder?** Yes, but only with prior permission of the pastor.

Will contributions to the church be collected at the ceremony?
No.

AFTER THE CEREMONY

Is there usually a reception after the ceremony?
Yes. It may be held at the church where the ceremony is conducted or in a home or a catering hall. Depending on the choice of the couple and of the bride's family, a full-course meal may be served. Alcoholic beverages are rarely served. There may be music and dancing. The reception may last more than two hours.

Would it be considered impolite to neither eat nor drink?
Yes.

Is there a grace or benediction before eating or drinking?
Possibly.

Is there a grace or benediction after eating or drinking?
Possibly. If guests arrive and start eating at different times, grace may be said after the meal.

Is there a traditional greeting for the family?
Offer your congratulations when you meet the family in the reception line after the service.

Is there a traditional form of address for clergy who may be at the reception?
"Pastor" or "Reverend."

Is it okay to leave early?
Yes.

5

Buddhist

HISTORY AND BELIEFS

Buddhism was founded in the sixth century B.C. in northern India by Siddhartha Gautama, who was born as the son to a king in what is now southern Nepal. Warned by a sage that his son would become either an ascetic or a universal monarch, the king confined his son to home. A few years after marrying and having a child of his own, Siddhartha escaped from his father's palace around the age of 29. Since he had been sheltered for his entire life from the pains of life, he was shocked when he beheld three men. The first was old and weak; the second was ill and diseased; the last was dead. Each represented different aspects of the impermanence inherent in all forms of earthly existence. He also saw a religious ascetic, who represented the possibility of a solution to these frailties.

Wandering in search of peace, Siddhartha tried many disciplines, including severe asceticism, until he came to the Bodhi Tree (the Tree of Enlightenment). He sat there in meditation until, at the age of 35, he became a Buddha, or one who is enlightened.

In his first sermon after achieving enlightenment, the Buddha spoke of the Four Noble Truths and the Noble Eightfold Path. These succinctly comprise the Buddha's insights into the essential ways of life and how to achieve spiritual liberation. The Buddha died at the age of 80. His last words were for his disciples not to depend on him, but on the *dharma*, or Buddhist teachings.

In subsequent centuries, Buddhism flowered in Asia. Asian immigrants to the United States from the early third of the 19th century to the present have brought Buddhism to America. The first significant influence of

Buddhist values and ideas on American intellectuals seems to have occurred in the 1830s in the writings of the New England transcendentalists. More recently, Buddhism has appealed to members of the Beat culture of the 1950s, the counterculture of the 1960s and the subsequent New Age movement.

In Canada, Buddhism may have arrived as early as the middle of the 19th century when the Chinese arrived, first from California and then from Hong Kong. World Buddhism (i.e., the many cultural Buddhisms from all over the world) began to impact on Canada only after the Canadian multiculturalism policy of the late 1960s. The three major Buddhist centers are Toronto, Vancouver and Montreal.

U. S. temples: Not available
U.S. membership: 500,000
(*data from the* 1993 Information Please Almanac)

Canadian temples: Not available
Canadian membership: 165,000+
(*data from* Stats Can, *1991*)

MARRIAGE CEREMONY

There is no standard Buddhist marriage ceremony in the United States or Canada. In some cases, the ceremony may be modeled after a standard Protestant wedding service. Regardless of the structure of the ceremony, the overall purpose is to remind those present of the essential Buddhist principle of non-harmfulness to all sentient beings.

The ceremony may last from 15 to 30 minutes.

BEFORE THE CEREMONY

Are guests usually invited by a formal invitation?
Guests will be invited orally, either in person or on the telephone, or through a written invitation.

If not stated explicitly, should one assume that children are invited?
The broad variables of Buddhist practice make this impossible to answer. Ask the couple or family members.

If one can't attend, what should one do?
RSVP with regrets. Ordinarily, no present is expected.

APPROPRIATE ATTIRE

Men: Standards for attire vary widely. A minority of temples expect men to wear a jacket and tie; the vast majority allow much more casual dress. Loose, comfortable, casual clothing is especially recommended for those temples in which members and guests sit on meditation cushions on the floor. (Guests are advised to call the temple prior to the service for details on seating.) No head covering is required in any Buddhist temple.

Women: A minority of temples expect a dress or a skirt and blouse. The vast majority allow more casual attire. Loose, comfortable, casual clothing is especially recommended for those temples in which members and guests sit on meditation cushions on the floor. (Guests are advised to call the temple prior to the service for details on seating.) Open-toed shoes and modest jewelry are permissible. No head covering is required in any Buddhist temple.

There are no rules regarding colors of clothing.

GIFTS

Is a gift customarily expected?
No.

Should gifts be brought to the ceremony?
See above.

THE CEREMONY

Where will the ceremony take place?
Either in a temple or outdoors.

When should guests arrive and where should they sit?
It is customary to arrive early. Where one sits depends on the particular tradition of that temple. Guests should be aware that a temple may have meditation cushions on the floor and not pews in which to sit.

If arriving late, are there times when a guest should *not* enter the ceremony?
Do not enter during meditation.

Are there times when a guest should *not* leave the ceremony?
No.

Who are the major officiants, leaders or participants at the ceremony and what do they do?

◆ *A minister or priest*, who officiates.
◆ *The bride and groom*.

What books are used?

There are no standard texts for Buddhist wedding ceremonies, although any readings will usually refer to kindness and compassion.

To indicate the order of the ceremony:

Since the ceremony is fairly brief and only the priest or monk does any recitations, there is little need to indicate the order of the event.

Will a guest who is not a Buddhist be expected to do anything other than sit?

Perhaps only to stand when others do.

Are there any parts of the ceremony in which a guest who is not a Buddhist should *not* participate?

No.

If not disruptive to the ceremony, is it okay to:

◆ **Take pictures?** Only with prior approval of a priest or monk.
◆ **Use a flash?** Only with prior approval of a priest or monk.
◆ **Use a video camera?** Only with prior approval of a priest or monk.
◆ **Use a tape recorder?** Only with prior approval of a priest or monk.

Will contributions to the temple be collected at the ceremony?

No.

AFTER THE CEREMONY

Is there usually a reception after the ceremony?

There may be a reception in the temple's reception area or at another site chosen by the newlyweds. Light food may be served, but not meat. There is usually no alcohol. The reception may last 60 minutes.

Would it be considered impolite to neither eat nor drink?

No.

Is there a grace or benediction before eating or drinking?

Possibly, depending on the particular Buddhist denomination and sect.

Is there a grace or benediction after eating or drinking?

Possibly, depending on the particular Buddhist denomination and sect.

Is there a traditional greeting for the family?

Just offer your congratulations.

Is there a traditional form of address for clergy who may be at the reception?

Depending on the particular Buddhist denomination, the form of address may be "Reverend," "Lama" or "Roshi."

Is it okay to leave early?

Yes.

6

Christian and Missionary Alliance

HISTORY AND BELIEFS

The Christian and Missionary Alliance is literally an *alliance* of evangelical believers, who have joined together, through their local churches and their own personal lives, to bring the gospel and the life of Jesus Christ to all peoples and all nations.

In the United States, the denomination has its roots in two groups—the Christian Alliance and the Evangelical Missionary Alliance—both of which were founded in 1887 by Dr. Albert B. Simpson, a Presbyterian minister motivated by the spiritual needs of urban residents in the United States, as well as by the unevangelized peoples in other lands. These two organizations' underlying thrust was Jesus' comment in Matthew (24:14): "The gospel of the kingdom will be preached in the whole world as a testimony to all nations, and then the end will come." In Canada, a movement that was begun in 1887 by Rev. John Salmon joined the Christian Alliance in 1889, becoming the Auxiliary of the Christian Alliance, Toronto.

The two groups that had been founded by Dr. Simpson were combined in 1897 to form the Christian and Missionary Alliance, which now has a worldwide membership of 2.4 million and ministries devoted to evangelism for Christ in 56 countries and territories. In 1981, the Canadian districts became autonomous and formed the Christian and Missionary Alliance in Canada. Its General Assembly is held every two years.

Presently, more than 1,169 missionaries are taking the Christian gospel to almost 150 "unsaved people groups" around the globe. The church defines a "people group" as "a distinct group of individuals having no community of Christians able to evangelize its people without outside help."

For example, the Church has two missionaries evangelizing Moslems residing in Great Britain, six to Chinese living in Australia, four to Native Americans living in urban areas in the United States, and two to North American Jews.

The Church believes that Jesus Christ is the living Word of God, the supreme Revelation of divine love, the sacrificial Lamb of God who alone provides salvation for humanity and every need of body and soul, and is the only hope for a world of lost people. Baptism and the Lord's Supper are recognized as the two ordinances of the Church. These are not related to individual salvation, but are outward signs of an inward commitment to Christ. Baptism by immersion is taught and practiced. The Lord's Supper is administered regularly in church services.

Church policies, which are set by an annual General Council, are administered by a 28-member Board of Managers and are implemented by the staff of the national office and district offices. Each local church sends its pastor and lay delegates to General Council and district conferences so it can have a voice in shaping policy.

U.S. churches: 1,850
U.S. membership: 311,600
(*data from the* 1998 Yearbook of American and Canadian Churches)

Canadian churches: 376
Canadian membership: 87,197
(*data from the* 1998 Yearbook of American and Canadian Churches)

MARRIAGE CEREMONY

Christian and Missionary Alliance churches affirm that God instructed that man and woman should marry when He said in Genesis (2:24), "For this reason a man will leave his father and mother and be united to his wife, and they will become one flesh."

In Matthew (19:6), Jesus quoted this passage from Genesis, adding, "Therefore, what God has joined together, let man not separate."

Genesis (2:18) further states, "It is not good that man should be alone." By this statement, God shows the incompleteness of man and woman apart from one another. Hence, marriage becomes the means to achieve completeness. From this physical and spiritual union, the home and family are established, which become the foundation of society and the well-being of the human race.

The 30- to 60-minute wedding service is a service in itself.

BEFORE THE CEREMONY

Are guests usually invited by a formal invitation?

Yes.

If not stated explicitly, should one assume that children are invited?

Yes.

If one can't attend, what should one do?

RSVP with regrets and send a gift.

APPROPRIATE ATTIRE

Men: Jacket and tie or more casual clothing. Standards and expectations for attire vary from church to church. No head covering is required.

Women: A dress. Hems need not reach below the knees nor must clothing cover the arms. Open-toed shoes and modest jewelry are permissible. No head covering is required.

There are no rules regarding colors of clothing.

GIFTS

Is a gift customarily expected?

Yes. Cash, small household appliances, and household furnishings, such as sheets or towels are customary.

Should gifts be brought to the ceremony?

Yes.

THE CEREMONY

Where will the ceremony take place?

In the main sanctuary of the church.

When should guests arrive and where should they sit?

Arrive early. Ushers will advise you where to sit.

If arriving late, are there times when a guest should *not* enter the ceremony?

Do not enter when the bride and her wedding party are marching down the aisle.

Are there times when a guest should *not* leave the ceremony?

Do not leave during the processional or recessional of the wedding party or during the recitation of the wedding vows.

Who are the major officiants, leaders or participants at the ceremony and what do they do?

- *The pastor,* who leads the service.
- *The bride and groom and members of the wedding party.*

What books are used?

A hymnal and Bible. The autonomy of individual churches precludes having standard hymnals and Bibles throughout the Church.

To indicate the order of the ceremony:

A program will be provided.

Will a guest who is not a member of the Christian and Missionary Alliance be expected to do anything other than sit?

No.

Are there any parts of the ceremony in which a guest who is not a member of the Christian and Missionary Alliance should *not* participate?

No.

If not disruptive to the ceremony, is it okay to:

- **Take pictures?** Yes.
- **Use a flash?** Sometimes, but only with prior permission of the pastor.
- **Use a video camera?** Yes.
- **Use a tape recorder?** Yes.

Will contributions to the church be collected at the ceremony?

No.

AFTER THE CEREMONY

Is there usually a reception after the ceremony?

Yes. This may last two hours or more. Anything from light snack food to a complete dinner will be served. Alcoholic beverages are not served.

Would it be considered impolite to neither eat nor drink?

No.

Is there a grace or benediction before eating or drinking?

Yes.

Is there a grace or benediction after eating or drinking?

Possibly.

Is there a traditional greeting for the family?

"Congratulations."

Is there a traditional form of address for clergy who may be at the reception?

"Pastor."

Is it okay to leave early?

Yes.

7

Christian Church (Disciples of Christ)

HISTORY AND BELIEFS

Reacting against the sectarianism common among religions on the American frontier of the early 1800s, the founders of the Christian Church urged a union of all Christians. Two independently developing groups, the "Disciples" and the "Christians," formally united in 1832.

They advocated adult baptism by immersion, weekly observance of the Lord's Supper (more commonly known as communion) and autonomy of local congregations.

The Canadian church traces its heritage to this new American group and to a similar movement within the Scotch Baptist movement in Britain.

One joins the Church after simply declaring his or her faith in Jesus and being baptized by immersion. The highly ecumenical Church was among the founders of the National and the World Councils of Churches. Its secular-oriented programs focus on such issues as helping the mentally retarded, aiding war victims, bolstering farms and improving cities and education.

The Church is highly democratic. Local congregations own their own property and control their budgets and programs. Each congregation votes in the General Assembly that meets every two years.

U.S. churches: 3,840
U.S. membership: 910,000
(*data from the* 1998 Yearbook of American and Canadian Churches)

Canadian churches: 34
Canadian membership: 3,286
(*data from the* 1998 Yearbook of American and Canadian Churches)

MARRIAGE CEREMONY

For Disciples of Christ, a church wedding is an act of worship in which the couple profess their love for and their commitment to each other before God and ask His blessing on their marriage. The same decorum exercised in any worship service should be exercised in the wedding service.

The wedding is a ceremony in itself. In it, the wedding party progresses in, then the pastor reads appropriate lessons from the Bible and asks the bride and groom about their commitment to one another. The pastor delivers a brief homily, wedding vows and rings are exchanged, and the couple are pronounced husband and wife.

The ceremony lasts between 15 and 30 minutes.

BEFORE THE CEREMONY

Are guests usually invited by a formal invitation?
Yes.

If not stated explicitly, should one assume that children are invited?
Yes.

If one can't attend, what should one do?
RSVP and send a gift.

APPROPRIATE ATTIRE

Men: Jacket and tie. No head covering is required.

Women: A dress, skirt and blouse, or pants suit are acceptable. Open-toed shoes and modest jewelry are fine. Neither a head covering nor hems below the knees are required.

There are no rules regarding colors of clothing.

GIFTS

Is a gift customarily expected?
Yes, ordinarily cash or items for the household such as small appliances, dishes, towels or blankets.

Should gifts be brought to the ceremony?
Either bring a gift to the ceremony and place it on the gift table or send it to the home of the newlyweds.

THE CEREMONY

Where will the ceremony take place?
In the main sanctuary of the House of Worship. The wedding party will stand near the altar in the chancel, the area in front of the sanctuary that includes the altar and pulpit and seating for clergy.

When should guests arrive and where should they sit?
It is appropriate to arrive before the time called for the ceremony. An usher will advise you where to sit.

If arriving late, are there times when a guest should *not* enter the ceremony?
Do not enter during the processional, recessional or during prayer.

Are there times when a guest should *not* leave the ceremony?
Do not leave during the processional, recessional or during prayer.

Who are the major officiants, leaders or participants at the ceremony and what do they do?
■ *The pastor*, who presides.
■ *The bride and groom and their wedding party.*

What books are used?
The New Revised Standard Version of the Bible (New York: National Council of Churches' Division of Christian Education, 1989) and the worship book with wedding liturgy.

To indicate the order of the ceremony:
Ushers will distribute a program.

Will a guest who is not a Disciple of Christ be expected to do anything other than sit?
The level of participation depends on whether or not the guest is Christian. Christians will generally be expected to stand and sing with congregants and read prayers aloud. Non-Christians are expected to stand with congregants and are invited to sing and pray with them.

Are there parts of the ceremony in which a guest who is not a Disciple of Christ should *not* participate?
No, unless they violate or compromise their own religious beliefs.

If not disruptive to the ceremony, is it okay to:
- **Take pictures?** Yes.
- **Use a flash?** Yes.
- **Use a video camera?** Yes.
- **Use a tape recorder?** Yes.

Will contributions to the church be collected at the ceremony?
No.

AFTER THE CEREMONY

Is there usually a reception after the ceremony?
Yes. It may be at the church, at home or in a catering hall. It may last between one to two hours. Food will be served. Alcoholic beverages may be served if the reception is not held at the church. There will probably be music and dancing.

Would it be considered impolite to neither eat nor drink?
No. If you have dietary restrictions, inform your host or hostess in advance.

Is there a grace or benediction before eating or drinking?
Guests should wait for the saying of grace before eating.

Is there a grace or benediction after eating or drinking?
No.

Is there a traditional greeting for the family?
Congratulate the new couple and their parents.

Is there a traditional form of address for clergy who may be at the reception?
"Pastor" or "Reverend."

Is it okay to leave early?
Yes.

8

Christian Congregation

(Also known as The Christian Church.
Since local churches are semi-autonomous, they are sometimes known as
Independents or Universalists. This latter term should not
be confused with Unitarian Universalism.)

HISTORY AND BELIEFS

The Christian Congregation originated in the late 18th century along the frontier near the Ohio River. It was incorporated in 1887 when several ministers formally constituted the Church because they sought greater cooperation with each other.

The Church considers itself to be a progressive organization that places greater emphasis on ethical behavior than on strict adherence to doctrine. Its guiding principle is John 13:34-35: "A new commandment I give to you, that you love one another, even as I have loved you, that you also love one another. By this, all men will know that you are My disciples, if you have love for one another." Essential to Church belief is the conviction that all wars are unjust, and that war itself is an obsolete means to resolve disputes. Its doctrinal positions are intended to transcend racial distinctions and national identities and to foster a creative activism.

The Christian Congregation is an evangelistic association whose local churches are semi-autonomous.

Number of U.S. churches: 1,437
Number of U.S. members: 114,700
(data from the 1998 Yearbook of American and Canadian Churches)

MARRIAGE CEREMONY

In the Christian Congregation, marriage is the uniting of a man and a woman in a union which is intended—and which is pledged—to be lifelong.

The marriage ceremony is a service in itself. It may last between 15 and 30 minutes.

BEFORE THE CEREMONY

Are guests usually invited by a formal invitation?

Yes.

If not stated explicitly, should one assume that children are invited?

Yes.

If one can't attend, what should one do?

RSVP with regrets.

APPROPRIATE ATTIRE

Men: A jacket and tie or slightly more casual attire. No head covering is required.

Women: A dress or a skirt and blouse or a pants suit. Shorts are not appropriate. Arms do not have to be covered nor do hems have to be below the knees. Open-toed shoes and modest jewelry are permissible. No head covering is required.

There are no rules regarding colors of clothing.

GIFTS

Is a gift customarily expected?

Yes, ordinarily cash or such items for the household as small appliances, dishes, towels or blankets.

Should gifts be brought to the ceremony?

Gifts are usually given to the newlyweds at the reception or are sent to their home.

THE CEREMONY

Where will the ceremony take place?

In the family's church.

When should guests arrive and where should they sit?

Arrive shortly before the time for which the service has been called. Ushers may be present to indicate where to sit. If not, sit wherever you wish.

If arriving late, are there times when a guest should *not* enter the ceremony?

Do not enter during prayers or during the processional or recessional.

Are there times when a guest should *not* leave the ceremony?

Do not leave during prayers or during the processional or recessional.

Who are the major officiants, leaders or participants at the ceremony and what do they do?

- *The minister,* who conducts the ceremony.
- *The bride and groom and their wedding party.*
- *The choir,* which sings.
- *The minister of music,* who directs the music.

What books are used?

Only the minister uses a book; guests do not.

To indicate the order of the ceremony:

A program will be provided and periodic announcements will be made by the minister.

Will a guest who is not a member of The Christian Congregation be expected to do anything other than sit?

No.

Are there any parts of the ceremony in which a guest who is not a member of The Christian Congregation should *not* participate?

No.

If not disruptive to the ceremony, is it okay to:

- **Take pictures?** Only with prior permission of the family.
- **Use a video camera?** Only with prior permission of the family.
- **Use a flash camera?** Only with prior permission of the family.
- **Use a tape recorder?** Only with prior permission of the family.

Will contributions to the church be collected at the ceremony?

No.

AFTER THE CEREMONY

Is there usually a reception after the ceremony?

Yes. This may be in the same building as the marriage ceremony, in a catering hall or in a home. It usually consists of light food, such as sandwiches, soft drinks and cookies, but never alcoholic beverages. The reception, which is an opportunity for fellowship and congratulating the newlyweds and taking their photos, may last about 60 minutes.

Would it be considered impolite to neither eat nor drink?

No.

Is there a grace or benediction before eating or drinking?

No.

Is there a grace or benediction after eating or drinking?

No.

Is there a traditional greeting for the family?

Just offer your congratulations.

Is there a traditional form of address for clergy who may be at the reception?

"Reverend." "Doctor" may be used if the minister has a Ph.D. or an honorary doctorate.

Is it okay to leave early?

Yes, but usually only after the wedding cake has been served.

9

Christian Science
(Church of Christ, Scientist)

HISTORY AND BELIEFS

Christian Science was founded in 1879 by Mary Baker Eddy, who was healed of a serious injury in 1866 while reading an account in the New Testament of Jesus' healings. Thirteen years later, she established the Church of Christ, Scientist, in Boston. Mrs. Eddy died in 1910.

The church consists of the Mother Church—the First Church of Christ, Scientist—in Boston and approximately 2,400 branch churches in about 63 countries around the world.

Christian Science theology holds that God created man in His image and likeness. Christian Scientists also believe that God is good and that His creation is all that is real and eternal. This belief is based on the first chapter of Genesis, which states: "So God created man in His own image, in the image of God created He him; male and female created He them.... And God saw everything that He had made, and, behold, it was good."

Therefore, Christian Scientists believe that sin, disease and death do not originate in God. Rather, they are considered to be distortions of the human mind.

The church is grounded in the teachings of the King James Bible and relies on spiritual means for healing. According to the church, its spiritual healing "is not popular faith healing or human mind cure. It is not self-hypnosis, mere positive thinking, autosuggestion, or spontaneous remission. Nor is it to be confused with Scientology or New Age thinking....

"Christian Scientists find the Christian healing they experience is the reinstatement of the healing method practiced by Jesus 2,000 years ago. It is based on understanding the laws of God revealed in the Bible, and conforming to them. These laws are available for all mankind to practice and, thereby, obtain full salvation from sickness as well as sin.

"Christian Science healing involves more than healing sick bodies. It heals broken hearts and minds as well as broken homes, and is directly applicable to all of society's ills."

U.S. churches: 2,400
U.S. membership: Not available
(*data from the* 1998 Yearbook of American and Canadian Churches)

Canadian churches: 94
Canadian membership: Not available

MARRIAGE CEREMONY

There is no set marriage ceremony. Since Christian Science has no ordained clergy, it has no one who can legally perform a marriage. In accord with the laws where they reside, Christian Scientists may be married by the clergy of another faith.

10

Church of the Brethren

HISTORY AND BELIEFS

The Church of the Brethren began in 1708 in an obscure German princi-
pality, Sayn-Wittgenstein-Hohenstein, when five men and three women
pledged to base their lives on biblical lessons and truths and "to take up all
the commandments of Jesus Christ as an easy yoke." They criticized the
Church as inattentive to the Bible and too concerned with maintaining
itself as an institution. They also believed that baptism was not for infants,
but for believers who had reached a mature age of accountability and
could decide for themselves to embrace Christian precepts.

By denying the validity of the baptism each member of this small group
had received as infants, they implicitly challenged the authority of the
existing Church. Since churches in Germany were closely identified with
the state, adult baptism was considered to be not only religious heresy, but
also treason. Soon, members of this expanding group were persecuted by
the state, not only for their stance on baptism, but also because they
refused to take oaths or serve in the military.

In 1719, some Brethren fled Europe for Pennsylvania. Four years later,
the entire male membership in the Germantown, Pennsylvania, congregation began an evangelistic mission to preach, baptize and form new congregations throughout the colonies. By the middle of the next century, there
were new churches as far as California.

The original members of the Church in Germany had simply called themselves "brethren," which meant brothers and sisters. But in 1836, legal papers
in the United States listed the group as the Fraternity of German Baptists.

This became the German Baptist Brethren in 1871, although they were also nicknamed "Dunkers" because of adult baptism by immersion.

In 1908, the German identification disappeared and the name was changed to the Church of the Brethren. There have been recent murmurings about again changing the Church's name since "brethren" generally refers only to males in today's usage. For now, "brethren" is being retained to remind members of the deep connections they have—as sisters and brothers—in their faith.

Church members affirm their belief in Jesus Christ as the Lord and Savior and promise to turn from sin and live in faithfulness to God and to the Church, taking Jesus as their model. The Church insists that members not thoughtlessly adopt the habits and ways of others, and encourages members to think carefully about how to live comfortably, but not ostentatiously, in an affluent society; to be aware of the environment and limited resources in a global community; and to engage in creative efforts to achieve peace and reconciliation. The Church condemns gambling and urges members to refrain from alcohol, drug and tobacco use. Brethren are encouraged to practice nonresistance in the face of violence, and discouraged from engaging in military service since the Church has declared all war to be sin.

Oath-taking is discouraged because the Church of the Brethren believes that Jesus advocated completely abolishing such practices (James 5:12) since persons should always be truthful, not just at particular moments. Taking an oath implies an erratic attitude toward truthfulness since it suggests that, this time, one is being truthful, yet is not truthful at other times. Jesus, according to the Church, taught that a true Christian knows the will of God and is true to it at all times. Indecisiveness, which is fostered by the devil, erodes one's credibility.

The Church also discourages members from resorting to civil court when injured by another because, as Peter Nead, the leading Brethren theologian of the 19th century, wrote, the doctrine taught by Jesus does not allow Christians "to retaliate or seek redress for their grievances. Under the law, retaliation was allowable, but not so under the Gospel of Jesus Christ." Instead, wrote Nead, when a Christian is injured by another, his only recourse is to suffer since that is what Jesus did and that is what anyone wishing to be a child of God must do.

But in a statement written in 1920, the Church slightly relaxed its proscription against members participating in proceedings in a civil court. The statement cited Matthew 5:40-41 and Luke 6:30 to show that Jesus taught that if the legal process cannot be avoided, then the Christian should do more than is required by secular law. The statement gave permission to Brethren to comply with civil law if three preconditions were met: Such action did not violate such Christian principles as nonresistance; one Brethren had not resorted to civil law without the permission of another Brethren whom he was contesting in a court action; and the Church's counsel is sought before resorting to civil law.

At least once a year, each church celebrates a "love feast," which may also be called an "agape (pronounced 'ah-GAH-pay') meal." The ceremony includes a mutual footwashing between two congregants of the same gender, who then embrace and give each other a "holy kiss." This is followed by communion and a simple meal. The ritual echoes Jesus' washing of the feet of His disciples at the Last Supper, where He sought to draw them closer into the fold of His love.

Individual Brethren congregations have considerable autonomy. Each sets its own budget and chooses its own pastor, a moderator who conducts the gatherings when Brethren meet to do church business, and a board of administration. Each also belongs to one of the 23 districts that comprise the Annual Conference, which meets each year to make decisions about the future of the Church. Each church can send at least one delegate to the conference.

U.S. churches: 1,106
U.S. membership: 141,800
(*data from the* 1998 Yearbook of American and Canadian Churches)

MARRIAGE CEREMONY

For the Church of the Brethren, a wedding ceremony recognizes the commitment of two people who agree to love each other faithfully and to live together within God's love to their mutual benefit. God joins the couple, but those who attend the wedding agree, by their presence, to offer them encouragement and support.

The wedding ceremony is a ceremony in itself. It may last from 30 to 60 minutes.

BEFORE THE CEREMONY

Are guests usually invited by a formal invitation?
Yes.

If not stated explicitly, should one assume that children are invited?
Yes.

If one can't attend, what should one do?

RSVP with regrets.

APPROPRIATE ATTIRE

Men: A jacket and tie or more casual attire, depending on local custom. No head covering is required.

Women: A dress or a skirt and blouse or a pants suit. Hems need not reach below the knees nor must clothing cover the arms. Open-toed shoes and modest jewelry are permissible. Some congregations prefer that a small head covering be worn. Traditionally, this "prayer covering" is a symbol of prayer and submission for women. It relates to Paul's admonition in I Corinthians 5-7, which states, in part, "...Every woman who has her head uncovered while praying or prophesying disgraces her head." Nevertheless, in recent years, increasingly fewer women have worn "prayer coverings." In those churches where head coverings are still customary, they will not be provided by the church. Guests may want to bring their own head covering—a scarf or small hat.

There are no rules regarding colors of clothing.

GIFTS

Is a gift customarily expected?

Usually, unless stipulated otherwise.

Should gifts be brought to the ceremony?

Local customs vary, but it is always correct to send gifts to the bride's home in advance of the wedding.

THE CEREMONY

Where will the ceremony take place?

Locations vary. The ceremony may be in a church, a home or outdoors.

When should guests arrive and where should they sit?

Arrive shortly before the time for which the ceremony has been called. Ushers will advise guests where to sit.

If arriving late, are there times when a guest should *not* enter the ceremony?

Do not enter during the processional of the wedding party or while prayers or marriage vows are being recited.

Are there times when a guest should *not* leave the ceremony?

Do not leave during the prayers or marriage vows or the recessional of the wedding party.

Who are the major officiants, leaders or participants at the ceremony and what do they do?

- *The pastor(s),* who officiates at the ceremony and witnesses the vows of the bride and groom.
- *The bride and groom and their wedding party.*
- *An instrumentalist, a vocalist and/or a choir.*

What books are used?

Since each congregation chooses the translation of the Bible it will use, different translations are used throughout the Church. Among the more common translations used is the New Revised Standard Version. Texts also used in services are a worship bulletin published by the local church, and *Hymnal: A Worship Book* (Elgin, Ill.: Brethren Press, 1992).

To indicate the order of the ceremony:

A program will usually be distributed or there will be periodic instructions by the pastor.

Will a guest who is not a member of the Church of the Brethren be expected to do anything other than sit?

It is expected for each guest to stand, sing and read prayers aloud with other guests if these do not violate their religious beliefs.

Are there any parts of the ceremony in which a guest who is not a member of the Church of the Brethren should *not* participate?

No.

If not disruptive to the ceremony, is it okay to:

- **Take pictures?** Only with prior permission of the family and pastor.
- **Use a flash?** No.
- **Use a video camera?** Only with prior permission of the family and pastor.
- **Use a tape recorder?** Only with prior permission of the family and pastor.

Will contributions to the church be collected at the ceremony?

No.

AFTER THE CEREMONY

Is there usually a reception after the ceremony?

There is usually a reception. This may be held in the church reception hall, in a catering hall or at a home. There may be light food served or a complete meal, but no alcoholic beverages if the reception is held in a church building. There may be a nonalcoholic toast to the newlyweds, and sometimes music and possibly dancing. Gifts are sometimes opened at the reception, which may last for one to two hours.

Would it be considered impolite to neither eat nor drink?

No.

Is there a grace or benediction before eating or drinking?

Grace is usually said.

Is there a grace or benediction after eating or drinking?

No.

Is there a traditional greeting for the family?

Just offer your congratulations.

Is there a traditional form of address for clergy who may be at the reception?

"Pastor."

Is it okay to leave early?

Yes.

11

Church of the Nazarene

HISTORY AND BELIEFS

The distant roots of Church of the Nazarene are in Methodism; its more recent roots are in the teachings of John Wesley, who led a revival centered on the doctrines of holiness and sanctification in 18th-century England; and its most recent roots are in three churches that merged in 1907 and 1908: The Association of Pentecostal Churches, which was based in New York and New England; the Holiness Church of Christ, which was based in the South; and the Church of the Nazarene, based in California.

The Church's doctrine centers on "sanctification," which is a feeling of grace stemming from "regeneration." This latter term refers to the sense of being made anew through faith in Jesus Christ. All pastors (who may also be called "ministers") and local church officials must profess this experience. Other prime doctrines are that the Scriptures contain all truths necessary to Christian faith and living; that through His death, Christ atoned for the sins of humanity; and that upon Christ's return, the dead will be resurrected.

Tobacco and alcohol use are prohibited. Church members believe in divine healing, but not to the exclusion of medical aid.

Each of the Church's 85 districts in the United States and Canada is supervised by a district superintendent, who is elected for a four-year term by members of the district assembly. Internationally, the Church is administered by a general board, which consists of an equal number of lay members and ministers.

The Church emphasizes evangelism, and more than 650 missionaries conduct missionary work around the globe.

Worldwide, there are almost 850,000 Nazarenes (as members of the Church of the Nazarene are called) in more than 8,600 churches.

U.S. churches: 5,135
U.S. membership: 608,000
(*data from the* 1998 Yearbook of American and Canadian Churches)

Canadian churches: 182
Canadian membership: 11,931
(*data from the* 1998 Yearbook of American and Canadian Churches)

MARRIAGE CEREMONY

In the Church of the Nazarene, marriage is the uniting of a man and a woman in a union which is intended—and which is pledged—to be lifelong.

The marriage ceremony is a service in itself. It may last between 15 and 30 minutes.

BEFORE THE CEREMONY

Are guests usually invited by a formal invitation?

Yes, although sometimes the invitation to the wedding may also be published in the church bulletin.

If not stated explicitly, should one assume that children are invited?

Yes.

If one can't attend, what should one do?

RSVP with regrets and send a gift if you have received a formal invitation to the wedding.

APPROPRIATE ATTIRE

Men: A suit and tie or a sport jacket, slacks and a tie. No head covering is required.

Women: A dress or a business suit appropriate to the season and the time of day for which the wedding has been called. Arms do not have to be covered nor do hems need to reach below the knees. Open-toed shoes and modest jewelry are permissible. No head covering is required.

There are no rules regarding colors of clothing.

GIFTS

Is a gift customarily expected?

Only if you have received a formal invitation to the wedding. Such gifts as small household appliances, sheets or towels or other household goods are appropriate.

Should gifts be brought to the ceremony?

Gifts may be brought to the ceremony itself, to the reception afterward or sent to the home of the newlyweds.

THE CEREMONY

Where will the ceremony take place?

In the church chapel or sanctuary.

When should guests arrive and where should they sit?

Arrive shortly before the time for which the wedding has been called and in time to sign the guest registry, which will be in the church foyer. Ushers will advise you where to sit.

If arriving late, are there times when a guest should *not* enter the ceremony?

Ushers will advise you about when to enter the service.

Are there times when a guest should *not* leave the ceremony?

Do not leave during the processional or recessional of the wedding party.

Who are the major officiants, leaders or participants at the ceremony and what do they do?

- *The pastor(s).*
- *The bride and groom and members of their wedding party.*

What books are used?

Only the pastor uses a text.

To indicate the order of the ceremony:

A program may be distributed.

Will a guest who is not a Nazarene be expected to do anything other than sit?

While it is customary for all guests to stand for the bride's entrance, they should stand only if the mother of the bride stands.

Are there any parts of the ceremony in which a guest who is not a Nazarene should *not* participate?

No.

If not disruptive to the ceremony, is it okay to:

- **Take pictures?** Only with prior permission of the pastor.
- **Use a flash?** Only with prior permission of the pastor.
- **Use a video camera?** Only with prior permission of the pastor.
- **Use a tape recorder?** Only with prior permission of the pastor.

Will contributions to the church be collected at the ceremony?

No.

AFTER THE CEREMONY

Is there usually a reception after the ceremony?

Yes. It may be held at any location chosen by the couple, possibly the church fellowship hall, a catering hall, a country club or a garden setting at a home. Light food, such as punch and cookies or cake, may be served. In some instance, there may be a full meal, but never alcoholic beverages. The reception may last up to two hours.

Would it be considered impolite to neither eat nor drink?

No.

Is there a grace or benediction before eating or drinking?

No.

Is there a grace or benediction after eating or drinking?

No.

Is there a traditional greeting for the family?

Just offer your congratulations.

Is there a traditional form of address for clergy who may be at the reception?

"Pastor."

Is it okay to leave early?

Yes.

12

Churches of Christ

HISTORY AND BELIEFS

Churches of Christ are autonomous congregations; there are no central governing offices or officers, and Church publications and institutions are either under local congregational control or independent of any one congregation. Members of the Churches of Christ appeal to the Bible alone to determine matters involving their faith and practice.

In the 19th century, Churches of Christ shared a common fellowship with the Christian Churches/Churches of Christ and with the Christian Church (Disciples of Christ). This relationship became strained after the Civil War because of emerging theories of interpreting the Bible and the centralizing of church-wide activities through a missionary society.

The Church teaches that Jesus Christ was divine, that the remission of sins can be achieved only by immersing oneself into Christ, and that the Scriptures were divinely inspired.

U.S. churches: 14,000
U. S. membership: 2.25 million
(*data from the* 1998 Yearbook of American and Canadian Churches)

Canadian churches: 145
Canadian membership: 6,950
(*data from the* 1998 Yearbook of American and Canadian Churches)

MARRIAGE CEREMONY

The Churches of Christ teaches that marriage "originated in the mind of God," who "created woman especially to be a companion for the man.... There can be no doubt that God intended for man and woman to marry," since God said, "For this cause shall a man leave his father and mother, and shall cleave unto his wife."

God "officiated" at the marriage between Adam and Eve, and "continues to officiate at all scriptural marriages today."

This is why the Church states that marriage is "divine" and that "those who marry not only have obligations to each other, but they also have obligations to God."

Usually, Churches of Christ marriage ceremonies last about 30 minutes.

BEFORE THE CEREMONY

Are guests usually invited by a formal invitation?
Yes. Often, general invitations are published in the church bulletin.

If not stated explicitly, should one assume that children are invited?
Yes.

If one can't attend, what should one do?
RSVP by phone or card, along with your congratulations. Most friends will send a gift either to a wedding shower or to the couple.

APPROPRIATE ATTIRE

Men: Jacket and tie, although occasionally less formal clothes may be suitable. No head covering is required.

Women: Dress modestly. Hems slightly above the knees are fine. Open-toed shoes and modest jewelry permissible. No head covering is required, but hats or scarfs may be worn.

There are no rules regarding colors of clothing.

GIFTS

Is a gift customarily expected?
Yes, either for the bridal shower or the wedding itself. Such gifts as small household appliances, sheets or towels or other household goods are appropriate.

Should gifts be brought to the ceremony?

If you bring a gift to the wedding, place it on the table in the reception area for that purpose. Gifts can also be sent to the home of the newlyweds.

THE CEREMONY

Where will the ceremony take place?

In the main sanctuary of the church.

When should guests arrive and where should they sit?

Arrive early. Sit wherever you wish.

If arriving late, are there times when a guest should *not* enter the ceremony?

Do not enter the service during the processional.

Are there times when a guest should *not* leave the ceremony?

Do not leave during the processional.

Who are the major officiants, leaders or participants at the ceremony and what do they do?

◪ *The minister*, who performs the ceremony.
◪ *Singers*.
◪ *The bride and groom and their wedding party.*

What books are used?

Usually, the minister has a Bible, from which he reads. Other books are usually not used.

To indicate the order of the ceremony:

A program will be provided.

Will a guest who is not a member of the Churches of Christ be expected to do anything other than sit?

Guests are only expected to enjoy the celebration.

Are there any parts of the ceremony in which a guest who is not a member of the Churches of Christ should *not* participate?

No.

If not disruptive to the ceremony, is it okay to:

◪ **Take pictures?** Yes.
◪ **Use a flash?** Yes.
◪ **Use a video camera?** Yes.
◪ **Use a tape recorder?** Yes.

Will contributions to the church be collected at the ceremony?

No.

AFTER THE CEREMONY

Is there usually a reception after the ceremony?
There is often a reception in the same building as the ceremony. It lasts about one hour. There may be finger foods, fruit, vegetables and dip. Alcohol in any form is discouraged, as is smoking inside the building.

Would it be considered impolite to neither eat nor drink?
No.

Is there a grace or benediction before eating or drinking?
Sometimes a prayer is said before eating.

Is there a grace or benediction after eating or drinking?
No. But usually after the reception, rice or bird seed are thrown at the newlyweds when they leave. (Bird seed has generally replaced rice because of ecological concerns.)

Is there a traditional greeting for the family?
No, just offer your congratulations.

Is there a traditional form of address for clergy who may be at the reception?
Churches of Christ do not have titles for clergy. Ministers or preachers are addressed no differently than are lay members. All church members are considered to be living lives of integrity and each should be trying to live a life as holy as the minister.

13

Episcopalian and Anglican

HISTORY AND BELIEFS

The Episcopal/Anglican Church is derived from the Church of England and shares with it traditions of faith as set forth in its *Book of Common Prayer*.

The English settlers who settled in Jamestown, Virginia, in 1607 brought the seeds of the Episcopal Church to America. After the American Revolution, the Church became independent from the Anglican Church and adopted the name of the Protestant Episcopal Church in the United States of America. This was shortened in 1967 when the Episcopal Church became the Church's official alternate name.

To many Americans after the Revolution, the Church was suspect because it had been closely linked with the British Crown and because many of its leaders and members had sided with England during the war. But extensive missionary efforts in the fledgling nation's new territories (as well as in Africa, Latin America and the Far East) and an eventual network of dioceses from the Atlantic to the Pacific helped it to finally establish its own identity.

In Canada, the first known service was performed by a chaplain in Sir Martin Frobisher's expedition in Frobisher Bay on September 2, 1578. In subsequent years, Anglicanism spread as a result of immigration from the British Isles and the coming of Loyalists, many of whom were Anglicans, after the American Revolution.

The Church is a fairly non-doctrinaire institution. It teaches that the Holy Scriptures were written by people, and inspired by the Holy Spirit (the empowering spirit of God), and that reason helps members penetrate to the full depths of God's truths. It does not control interpretation and practice, and urges members to make responsible moral decisions under the guidance of scripture, tradition and ordained ministry and in response to sincere prayer.

The Episcopal/Anglican Church is democratically structured. Each diocese, which consists of a group of parishes (or churches), is presided over by a bishop, who is democratically elected by a diocesan synod.

According to *The Book of Common Prayer*, "the duty of all Christians is to follow Christ, to come together week by week for corporate worship; and to work, pray and give for the spread of the Kingdom of God."

U.S. churches: 7,415
U.S. membership: 2.5 million
(*data from the* 1998 Yearbook of American and Canadian Churches)

Canadian churches: 2,390
Canadian membership: 740,262

MARRIAGE CEREMONY

The Episcopal/Anglican Church believes that, through the sacrament of marriage, God joins together man and woman in physical and spiritual union.

The marriage ceremony may either be a ceremony in itself or part of a Holy Communion service. It may last between 30 and 60 minutes.

BEFORE THE CEREMONY

Are guests usually invited by a formal invitation?
Yes.

If not stated explicitly, should one assume that children are invited?
No.

If one can't attend, what should one do?
RSVP with your regrets and send a gift.

APPROPRIATE ATTIRE

Men: Jacket and tie or more casual clothing (depending on the style of the wedding. This may be indicated in the invitation.) No head covering required.

Women: Dress or a skirt and blouse or a pants suit. Open-toed shoes and jewelry are permissible. No head covering required.

There are no rules regarding colors of clothing.

GIFTS

Is a gift customarily expected?

Yes, costing between $20 and $40.

Should gifts be brought to the ceremony?

Yes, or they can be sent to the home.

THE CEREMONY

Where will the ceremony take place?

Depending on the wishes of the couple being married, it may be in the main sanctuary of a church, in another part of the church, in a home or banquet hall, or in another setting of their choice.

When should guests arrive and where should they sit?

Arrive early. Depending on the setting, ushers may show guests where to sit.

If arriving late, are there times when a guest should *not* enter the ceremony?

Check with the ushers.

Are there times when a guest should *not* leave the ceremony?

Guests should plan to remain for the entire service.

Who are the major officiants, leaders or participants at the ceremony and what do they do?

Depending on the setting and the wishes of the couple, there may be:

◗ *A priest*, who presides, preaches and celebrates communion.
◗ *A lector*, who reads from the Old Testament and/or the Epistles or apostolic letters, which are a part of the New Testament.
◗ *A deacon*, who reads the Gospel, which records the life and ministry of Jesus.
◗ *A lay minister*, or chalicist, who assists with the distribution of communion.
◗ *An intercessor*, who reads the "prayers of the people," which are petitions, intercessions and thanksgivings by the congregation.
◗ *The bride and groom and their wedding party.*

What books are used?

The Book of Common Prayer (New York: Church Hymnal Corp., 1986) and a hymnal. In Canada, *The Book of Alternative Services* (Toronto: The Anglican Book Center, 1985) may be used. Occasionally, the Bible lessons are included in the program.

To indicate the order of the ceremony:
A program will be provided.

Will a guest who is not Episcopalian/Anglican be expected to do anything other than sit?
They are expected to stand and kneel with the congregation, read prayers aloud and sing with congregants, if this does not compromise their personal beliefs. If one does not wish to kneel, sit when congregants do so. The only behavior that would be considered "offensive" would be not to stand for the reading of the Gospel.

Are there any parts of the ceremony in which a guest who is not Episcopalian/Anglican should *not* participate?
Do not receive communion or say any prayers contradictory to the beliefs of your own faith. Only baptized Christians may receive communion.

If not disruptive to the ceremony, is it okay to:
- **Take pictures?** No.
- **Use a flash?** No.
- **Use a video camera?** No.
- **Use a tape recorder?** No.

(Photos and videos are usually taken after the ceremony.)

Will contributions to the church be collected at the ceremony?
No.

AFTER THE CEREMONY

Is there usually a reception after the ceremony?
There is usually a reception that may last one to two hours. It may be at a home or at a catering facility. Food and beverages may be served and there may be dancing and music.

Would it be considered impolite to neither eat nor drink?
No.

Is there a grace or benediction before eating or drinking?
Not normally, but there may be a blessing if the reception is a "sit-down" affair.

Is there a grace or benediction after eating or drinking?
No.

Is there a traditional greeting for the family?

Extend your congratulations and best wishes.

Is there a traditional form of address for clergy who may be at the reception?

"Mr.," "Miss" or "Mrs." is usually sufficient.

Is it okay to leave early?

Yes, but usually only after toasts have been made and the wedding cake is cut and served.

14

Evangelical Free Church

HISTORY AND BELIEFS

The Evangelical Free Church is an association of autonomous churches that are united by a commitment to serve Jesus Christ. "Evangelical" refers to Church members' commitment to the proclamation of the Gospel and the authority of the Scriptures as the only sufficient guide to faith and practice. "Free" refers to the church government that assures local churches are independent of a central controlling body. Evangelical Free Churches depend upon the active participation of pastors and laity to make decisions that direct their local church.

The Evangelical Free Church of America was formed in 1950 by the merger of the Swedish Evangelical Free Church and the Norwegian-Danish Evangelical Free Church Association. The two denominations had a total of 275 local churches, and both had originated in the revival movements of the late nineteenth century.

A partner Church, The Evangelical Free Church of Canada, also of Scandinavian heritage, was incorporated under federal charter in 1967, although it traces its history to Enchant, Alberta, where the first formally organized congregation opened its doors in 1917.

From its inception, the Evangelical Free Church has been committed to being actively involved in the mission of Jesus Christ. Internationally, this dates from one of its two original Churches—the Swedish Evangelical Free Church—sending their first missionaries to China in 1887.

The Evangelical Free Church has national church bodies in 16 nations and plans to expand to another 15 countries. Domestically, the Church is committed to "planting" 1,000 new local churches by the year 2001.

77

U.S. churches: 1,224
U.S. membership: 242,619

(*data from the* 1998 Yearbook of American and Canadian Churches)

Canadian churches: 135
Canadian membership: 7,315

(*data from the* Evangelical Free Church of Canada 1998–1999 Directory)

MARRIAGE CEREMONY

In the Evangelical Free Church, marriage is considered to be a sacred union since it is an institution ordained by God in Genesis and affirmed by Jesus in the Gospels. The sacredness of the marriage ceremony and the relationship between man and wife are based upon the Scriptures and the teaching that marriage represents our relationship to Jesus Christ.

The wedding ceremony usually lasts between 30 and 60 minutes. It is a service in itself.

BEFORE THE CEREMONY

Are guests usually invited by a formal invitation?
Yes.

If not stated explicitly, should one assume that children are invited?
No.

If one can't attend, what should one do?
RSVP with regrets and send a gift to the newlyweds.

APPROPRIATE ATTIRE

Men: A jacket and tie. No head covering is required.

Women: A dress or a skirt and blouse. Open-toed shoes and modest jewelry are permissible. Clothing need not cover the arms nor hems reach below the knees. No head covering is required.

There are no rules regarding colors of clothing.

GIFTS

Is a gift customarily expected?
Cash or U.S. savings bonds or small household items are most frequently given.

Should gifts be brought to the ceremony?

Gifts may be brought to the ceremony, to the reception afterward or sent to the home of the newlyweds.

THE CEREMONY

Where will the ceremony take place?

The ceremony may be in the main sanctuary of the church or in another appropriate setting, such as a catering hall or even outdoors.

When should guests arrive and where should they sit?

Arrive early. Ushers will advise guests about where to sit.

If arriving late, are there times when a guest should *not* enter the ceremony?

Do not enter during the processional by the wedding party.

Are there times when a guest should *not* leave the ceremony?

Do not leave until the service is over.

Who are the major officiants, leaders or participants at the ceremony and what do they do?

- *The pastor,* who performs the ceremony.
- *The bride and groom and members of their wedding party.*

What books are used?

Instead of hymnals, most churches use overhead projectors to project the words of hymns for guests to sing.

To indicate the order of the ceremony:

A program will be provided.

Will a guest who is not a member of the Evangelical Free Church be expected to do anything other than sit?

Stand with the other guests. It is entirely optional for non-church members to sing and read prayers aloud with church members.

Are there any parts of the ceremony in which a guest who is not a member of the Evangelical Free Church should *not* participate?

No.

If not disruptive to the ceremony, is it okay to:

- **Take pictures?** Yes.
- **Use a flash?** No.

⊡ **Use a video camera?** Yes.
⊡ **Use a tape recorder?** Yes.

Will contributions to the church be collected at the ceremony?

No.

AFTER THE CEREMONY

Is there usually a reception after the ceremony?

Yes. This may be held in the church's reception hall, in a catering facility, in a home or outdoors. Food (often a complete meal) is usually served, although no alcoholic beverages will be served. There may be music, but no dancing. The length of the reception varies, but it may last two hours or more.

Would it be considered impolite to neither eat nor drink?

No.

Is there a grace or benediction before eating or drinking?

No.

Is there a grace or benediction after eating or drinking?

Possibly.

Is there a traditional greeting for the family?

"Congratulations."

Is there a traditional form of address for clergy who may be at the reception?

"Pastor."

Is it okay to leave early?

Yes.

15

Greek Orthodox

HISTORY AND BELIEFS

The Orthodox Church was essentially an outgrowth of the Great Schism over doctrinal issues between east and west in the Christian world in the year 1054. This caused a complete breakdown in communication between the Roman Catholic Church, based in Rome, and the Orthodox church, which remained under the jurisdiction of the Patriarch of Constantinople (present day Istanbul).

The word "Greek" is used not just to describe the Orthodox Christian people of Greece and others who speak Greek, but to refer to the early Christians who originally formed the initial Christian church and whose members spoke Greek and used Greek thought to find appropriate expressions of the Orthodox faith.

The term "Orthodox" is used to reflect adherents' belief that they believe and worship God correctly.

Essentially, Orthodox Christians consider their beliefs similar to those of other Christian traditions, but believe that the balance and integrity of the teachings of Jesus' twelve apostles have been preserved inviolate by their church.

Greek Orthodoxy holds that the eternal truths of God's saving revelation in Jesus Christ are preserved in the living tradition of the church under the guidance and inspiration of the Holy Spirit, which is the empowering spirit of God and the particular endowment of the church. While the Bible is the written testimony of God's revelation, Holy Tradition is the all-encompassing experience of the church under the guidance and direction of the Holy Spirit.

The first Greek Orthodox community in the Americas was founded in 1864 in New Orleans by a small colony of Greek merchants. In 1892, the first permanent community of Greek Orthodox in the United States was founded in New York. This is now known as the Archdiocesan Cathedral of the Holy Trinity and See of the Archbishop of North and South America.

There are now about seven million Orthodox Christians in the Western Hemisphere.

U.S. churches: 500
U.S. membership: 1.5 million
(data from the Greek Orthodox Diocese of America)

Canadian churches: 76
Canadian membership: 350,000
(data from the 1998 Yearbook of American and Canadian Churches)

MARRIAGE CEREMONY

To Greek Orthodox, marriage is a sacrament of union between man and woman, who enter it to be mutually complemented and to propagate the human race.

The 30- to 60-minute marriage ceremony is a ceremony in itself and not part of a larger service.

BEFORE THE CEREMONY

Are guests usually invited by a formal invitation?
Yes.

If not stated explicitly, should one assume that children are invited?
No.

If one can't attend, what should one do?
RSVP with regrets and send a gift.

APPROPRIATE ATTIRE

Men: Jacket and tie. A head covering is not required.

Women: A dress or a skirt and blouse. Clothing should cover the arms and hems should reach below the knees. A head covering is not required. Open-toed shoes and modest jewelry may be worn.

There are no rules regarding colors of clothing.

GIFTS

Is a gift customarily expected?

Yes. Appropriate gifts are cash or bonds valued at $50 to $500, or gifts chosen from bridal registries in shops.

Should gifts be brought to the ceremony?

They should be either sent to the home or brought to the reception and placed on the gift table.

THE CEREMONY

Where will the ceremony take place?

In the main sanctuary of the church chosen by the celebrants and their family.

When should guests arrive and where should they sit?

Arrive early. An usher will advise guests where to sit.

If arriving late, are there times when a guest should *not* enter the ceremony?

Do not enter during scripture readings and priestly blessings.

Are there times when a guest should *not* leave the ceremony?

No.

Who are the major officiants, leaders or participants at the ceremony and what do they do?

- *The priest*, who officiates.
- *The bride and groom.*
- *The best man and maid of honor*, who participate and assist during the ceremony.

What books are used?

Only the priest uses a book.

To indicate the order of the ceremony:

A program will be distributed.

Will a guest who is not Greek Orthodox be expected to do anything other than sit?

Yes. Stand when the congregation does.

Are there any parts of the ceremony in which a guest who is not Greek Orthodox should *not* participate?

No.

If not disruptive to the ceremony, is it okay to:
- **Take pictures?** Yes.
- **Use a flash?** Yes.
- **Use a video camera?** Yes.
- **Use a tape recorder?** Yes.

Will contributions to the church be collected at the ceremony?
No.

AFTER THE CEREMONY

Is there usually a reception after the ceremony?
There is often a formal reception lasting two hours or more. There will be a toast to the newlyweds, a meal, music and dancing. The reception may be in the same building as the ceremony, at the parents' home, or at a catering hall.

Would it be considered impolite to neither eat nor drink?
No.

Is there a grace or benediction before eating or drinking?
Yes. An invocation is recited to bless the food.

Is there a grace or benediction after eating or drinking?
No.

Is there a traditional greeting for the family?
Yes: "May you prosper." Or simply offer your congratulations.

Is there a traditional form of address for clergy who may be at the reception?
Yes: "Father."

Is it okay to leave early?
Yes, anytime.

16

Hindu

HISTORY AND BELIEFS

There are extraordinary differences between Hindu culture and beliefs and the prevailing Judeo-Christian religions and cultures in North America. Yet, from the Transcendentalists in New England in the early 19th century through the beatniks of the 1950s and the spiritual seekers of today, Hinduism has held a fascination for many thousands of North Americans. Most of these were either influenced tangentially by Hinduism or became actual practitioners of certain aspects of it for a while. But today, the vast majority of Hindus in the United States and Canada are immigrants from Asia, especially from India.

Unlike other religions, Hinduism has no founder and no common creed or doctrine. Generally, it teaches that God is both within being and object in the universe—and transcends every being and object; that the essence of each soul is divine; and that the purpose of life is to become aware of that divine essence. The many forms of worship ritual and meditation in Hinduism are intended to lead the soul toward direct experience of God or Self.

In general, the different gods and goddesses in Hinduism are different ways of conceiving and approaching the one God beyond name and form. Different forms of worship through images, symbols and rituals are helpful to different kinds of persons. Some do not need external worship. The goal is to transcend these forms and the world as it is ordinarily perceived and to realize the divine presence everywhere.

U.S. temples: Not available
U.S. membership: 1 million
(1995 data from The Vedanta Society)

85

Canadian temples: Not available
Canadian membership: 100,000+
(*data from the* 1992 Corpus Almanac & Canadian Sourcebook)

MARRIAGE CEREMONY

Hindu marriages are generally arranged by the parents or guardians of the bride and groom. In those rare cases where males and females choose their own partners, permission must be obtained from both sets of parents. No premarital dating or free mixing is allowed between males and females of marriageable age.

A Hindu marriage has seven major ceremonies:

- *Vagdana*, the verbal contract about the marriage between the fathers or guardians of the bride and groom.
- *Kanya Sampradana*, the giving away of the daughter to the groom by her father or guardian.
- *Varana*, welcoming the bride and groom.
- *Panigrahana*, ritualistic holding of each other's hands by the bride and groom.
- *Saptapadi*, a seven-step walking ritual by the bride and groom.
- *Laj homa,* creation of the holy fire that symbolizes the formless divinity. The bride and groom circle it four times and offer a parched paddy as oblation.
- *Sindur dam*, the groom puts red vermilion on the forehead and the furrow of the parted hair of the bride.

Marriage ceremonies are usually held after sunset and before sunrise.

BEFORE THE CEREMONY

Are guests usually invited by a formal invitation?
Yes.

If not stated explicitly, should one assume that children are invited?
Yes.

If one can't attend, what should one do?
RSVP with regrets and send a gift.

APPROPRIATE ATTIRE

Men: Dress casually. No head covering is required.

Women: Dress casually. Not required are a head covering, clothing that covers the arms or hems that reach below the knees. Open-toed shoes and modest jewelry are permissible.

There are no rules regarding colors of clothing.

GIFTS

Is a gift customarily expected?
Yes, usually household items.

Should gifts be brought to the ceremony?
Yes.

THE CEREMONY

Where will the ceremony take place?
In any area that is covered. This could be a temple, a home, a catering hall or outside under a canopy.

When should guests arrive and where should they sit?
Arrive at the time specified for the ceremony to begin. Sit wherever you wish.

If arriving late, are there times when a guest should *not* enter the ceremony?
No.

Are there times when a guest should *not* leave the ceremony?
No.

Who are the major officiants, leaders or participants at the ceremony and what do they do?
- *Priests*, who officiate.
- *Parents and/or guardians*, who exchange verbal contracts about the marriage. Also, the bride's father gives her to the groom.
- *Bride and groom.*

What books are used?
Only the priests use books.

To indicate the order of the ceremony:
Ordinarily, neither a program is distributed nor are periodic announcements made by the officiating priests. The ceremony just proceeds, although in the United States and Canada, the priest may occasionally explain the ceremony to guests who are not Hindus.

Will a guest who is not a Hindu be expected to do anything other than sit?
No.

Are there any parts of the ceremony in which a guest who is not a Hindu should *not* participate?
No.

If not disruptive to the ceremony, is it okay to:
- Take pictures? Yes.
- Use a flash? Yes.
- Use a video camera? Yes.
- Use a tape recorder? Yes.

Will contributions to the temple be collected at the ceremony?
No.

AFTER THE CEREMONY

Is there usually a reception after the ceremony?
There is a reception before and after the ceremony. Traditional Indian foods are served. It may last for many hours.

Would it be considered impolite to neither eat nor drink?
Yes.

Is there a grace or benediction before eating or drinking?
No.

Is there a grace or benediction after eating or drinking?
No.

Is there a traditional greeting for the family?
No. Just offer your "congratulations."

Is there a traditional form of address for clergy who may be at the reception?
"Swamiji" ("SWAH-mee-jee") if a monk, "Panditji" if a priest.

Is it okay to leave early?
Yes.

17

International Church of the Foursquare Gospel

HISTORY AND BELIEFS

The International Church of the Foursquare Gospel was founded in 1923 in Los Angeles by Aimee Semple McPherson. The new Church was an outgrowth of the revival movement in the United States that had begun at the turn of the century. Many involved in the movement spoke "in tongues" (in a language unknown to those speaking it), and claims were made of divine healing that saved lives. Since many of these experiences were associated with the coming of the Holy Spirit (the empowering quality of God) on the Day of Pentecost, participants in the revival were called Pentecostals.

"Foursquare" is a biblical term used in the Book of Exodus to refer to the tabernacle, in the Book of Ezekiel to refer to the Temple of the Lord, and in the Book of Revelation to refer to Heaven. Aimee Semple McPherson first used the term "Foursquare Gospel" during an evangelical campaign in Oakland, California, in 1922. It represents that which is equally balanced on all sides, and which is established and enduring. Such confidence in the power of the Gospel is also expressed by a New Testament verse (Hebrews 13:8) that is displayed in Foursquare churches: "Jesus Christ the Same, Yesterday, Today, and Forever."

The "Foursquare Gospel" presents Jesus Christ as Savior of the world, Baptizer with the Holy Spirit, the Great Physician, and the Soon-Coming King. It shares with the entire Pentecostal movement the concept that the truth of the Baptism is proven when the Holy Spirit empowers one to

89

speak in tongues. The Church also shares the core Pentecostal belief in bodily healing rooted in individual atonement.

Men and women participate equally at all levels of the Church.

Official business of the International Church of the Foursquare Gospel is conducted by a president, a board of directors that is called the Foursquare Cabinet and an executive council. The Church's highest authority is its annual convention, which has the sole authority to make or amend the Church's by-laws.

District supervisors are appointed by the president, with the approval of the board of directors for districts in the United States. They are ratified by the pastors of their respective districts every four years. The ministry of each local congregation is cared for by a pastor, a church council, deacons and deaconesses and elders. Each church is expected to contribute monthly to missionary work in the United States and abroad.

In Canada, a national church, the Foursquare Gospel Church of Canada, was formed in 1981.

The Church's strong emphasis on missionary work has produced more than 80 Hispanic churches in North America and at least four major churches that minister to African-Americans. Abroad, 17,226 congregations serve 1.8 million adherents.

U.S. churches: 1,773
U.S. membership: 229,600
(*data from the* 1998 Yearbook of American and Canadian Churches)

Canadian churches: 54
Canadian membership: 3,063
(*data from the* 1998 Yearbook of American and Canadian Churches)

MARRIAGE CEREMONY

The International Church of the Foursquare Gospel teaches that the family was the first institution ordained by God in the Garden of Eden. The basis for a family is marriage between a consenting adult male and female. Marriage, which is not to be entered into lightly, is said to be "until death do us part."

The marriage ceremony is a ceremony in itself and may last 30 to 60 minutes.

BEFORE THE CEREMONY

Are guests usually invited by a formal invitation?

Yes.

If not stated explicitly, should one assume that children are invited?

No.

If one can't attend, what should one do?

RSVP by card or letter with regrets and send a gift.

APPROPRIATE ATTIRE

Men: A jacket and tie. No head covering is required.

Women: A dress or a skirt and blouse. Clothing need not cover the arms and hems need not reach below the knees. Open-toed shoes and modest jewelry are permissible. No head covering is required.

There are no rules regarding colors of clothing.

GIFTS

Is a gift customarily expected?

Yes. Cash, savings bonds or small household items are frequently given.

Should gifts be brought to the ceremony?

Gifts may either be brought to the ceremony or the reception afterward, or sent to the home of the newlyweds.

THE CEREMONY

Where will the ceremony take place?

In the auditorium of the church.

When should guests arrive and where should they sit?

Arrive shortly before the time for which the ceremony has been called. Ushers will usually advise guests about where to sit.

If arriving late, are there times when one should *not* enter the ceremony?

Do not enter during the processional or recessional of the wedding party.

Are there times when a guest should *not* leave the ceremony?

Do not leave during the processional or recessional of the wedding party.

Who are the major officiants, leaders or participants at the ceremony and what do they do?

◘ *The pastor,* who officiates.
◘ *The bride and groom and members of the wedding party.*

What books are used?

None.

To indicate the order of the ceremony:

A program will be distributed.

Will a guest who is not a member of the International Church of the Foursquare Gospel be expected to do anything other than sit?

Stand when other guests arise during the ceremony.

Are there any parts of the ceremony in which a guest who is not a member of the International Church of the Foursquare Gospel should *not* participate?

No.

If not disruptive to the ceremony, is it okay to:

◘ **Take pictures?** Yes.
◘ **Use a flash?** Yes.
◘ **Use a video camera?** Yes.
◘ **Use a tape recorder?** Yes.

Will contributions to the church be collected at the ceremony?

No.

AFTER THE CEREMONY

Is there usually a reception after the ceremony?

Yes. It may be in the same building where the wedding ceremony was held or in a catering hall. Receptions usually include light food, such as cake, mints, nuts and punch. There will be no alcoholic beverages or dancing, although there might be music. The reception may last 30 to 60 minutes.

Would it be considered impolite to neither eat nor drink?

No.

Is there a grace or benediction before eating or drinking?

Yes.

Is there a grace or benediction after eating or drinking?

No.

Is there a traditional greeting for the family?

Just offer your congratulations.

Is there a traditional form of address for clergy who may be at the reception?

"Reverend."

Is it okay to leave early?

Yes.

18

International Pentecostal Holiness Church

HISTORY AND BELIEFS

The International Pentecostal Holiness Church has its origins in the first Pentecostal denominations in the United States: The Pentecostal Holiness Church, the Fire-Baptized Holiness Church, and the Tabernacle Pentecostal Church. The first two churches merged in 1911; the last church joined them in 1915. In Canada, it is known as the Pentecostal Holiness Church of Canada.

The Church emphasizes direct access to God, the Father; believes prayer can manifest miracles, especially divine healing; and is certain that the Holy Spirit may be evidenced during worship services by certain congregants speaking "in tongues," which are languages unknown to the speaker. The Church also teaches the imminent coming of Jesus Christ and that Jesus shed His blood for the complete cleansing of those who believe in Him from all indwelling sin.

Worldwide, the 12,802 churches of the International Pentecostal Holiness Church have 2.3 million members. The Church also has 155 missionaries in 80 countries.

The government of the Church gives individual churches a measure of denominational uniformity and local autonomy.

U.S. churches: 1,653
U.S. membership: 157,163
(*data from the* 1998 Yearbook of American and Canadian Churches)

94

Canadian churches: Not available
Canadian membership: 2,500
(data from the Pentecostal Holiness Church of Canada)

MARRIAGE CEREMONY

The International Pentecostal Holiness Church teaches that the family was the first institution ordained by God in the Garden of Eden. The basis for a family is marriage between two consenting adults. Marriage is said to be "until death do us part."

The marriage ceremony is a ceremony in itself and may last 30 to 60 minutes.

BEFORE THE CEREMONY

Are guests usually invited by a formal invitation?
Yes.

If not stated explicitly, should one assume that children are invited?
Yes.

If one can't attend, what should one do?
RSVP by card or letter with regrets and send a gift.

APPROPRIATE ATTIRE

Men: A jacket and tie. No head covering is required.

Women: A dress or a skirt and blouse or a pants suit. Clothing need not cover the arms and hems need not reach below the knees. Open-toed shoes and modest jewelry are permissible. No head covering is required.

There are no rules regarding colors of clothing.

GIFTS

Is a gift customarily expected?
Yes. Cash or U.S. savings bonds valued at $20 to $50 or small household items are most frequently given, as are any items listed in the newlyweds' gift registry.

Should gifts be brought to the ceremony?
Gifts may be brought to the ceremony or the reception afterward.

THE CEREMONY

Where will the ceremony take place?

In the sanctuary of the church.

When should guests arrive and where should they sit?

Arrive shortly before the time for which the ceremony has been called. Ushers will usually advise guests where to sit.

If arriving late, are there times when a guest should *not* enter the ceremony?

Do not enter during the processional or recessional of the wedding party.

Are there times when a guest should *not* leave the ceremony?

Do not leave during the processional or recessional of the wedding party.

Who are the major officiants, leaders or participants at the ceremony and what do they do?

- *The pastor,* who officiates.
- *The bride and groom and members of the wedding party.*
- *Musicians,* who provide special music.

What books are used?

None.

To indicate the order of the ceremony:

A program will be distributed and periodic announcements will be made by the minister.

Will a guest who is not a member of the International Pentecostal Holiness Church be expected to do anything other than sit?

No.

Are there any parts of the ceremony in which a guest who is not a member of the International Pentecostal Holiness Church should *not* participate?

No.

If not disruptive to the ceremony, is it okay to:

- **Take pictures?** No.
- **Use a flash?** No.
- **Use a video camera?** No.
- **Use a tape recorder?** Yes.

Will contributions to the church be collected at the ceremony?
No.

AFTER THE CEREMONY

Is there usually a reception after the ceremony?
Usually. It may be in the same building where the wedding ceremony was held or in a catering hall or in a private room at a hotel or restaurant. Receptions usually include light food, such as cake, nuts, hors d'oeuvres and punch. There will be no alcoholic beverages or dancing, although there might be music. The reception may last 30 to 60 minutes.

Would it be considered impolite to neither eat nor drink?
No.

Is there a grace or benediction before eating or drinking?
No.

Is there a grace or benediction after eating or drinking?
No.

Is there a traditional greeting for the family?
Just offer your congratulations.

Is there a traditional form of address for clergy who may be at the reception?
"Pastor" or "Reverend."

Is it okay to leave early?
Yes.

19

Islam

HISTORY AND BELIEFS

The Arabic word *Islam* means "submission," and Islam is the religion of submission to the will of God ("Allah" in Arabic).

Muhammad, who is regarded as the last and final prophet of Allah, was born in Mecca (in present-day Saudi Arabia) in approximately 570 A.D. As a young man, he sought solitude in a cave on the outskirts of Mecca, where, according to Muslim belief, he received revelation from God. The basic creed that Muhammad taught is that the one God in heaven demands morality and monotheistic devotion from those He has created.

Initially, Muhammad's message was widely rejected, especially by Mecca's elite, which felt threatened by its egalitarian teachings. But by the time he died in 632 A.D., most of Arabia had embraced Islam.

Muslims revere the Qur'an, their holy book, as the earthly cornerstone of their faith.

Islam teaches that the Hebrew Bible and the New Testament were also authentic revelations from God and recognizes as prophets all those mentioned as such in those scriptures, including Abraham, Moses, David and Jesus.

With about one billion Muslims around the globe, Islam is the fastest growing religion in the world. Every country in the world has at least a small Muslim community. There are now Muslims in nearly every town in the United States, with more substantial numbers in larger cities, especially in the East and Midwest and on the West Coast. In Canada, there are Muslims in every major city, with substantial numbers in the provinces of Ontario, Alberta and British Columbia.

U.S. mosques: 1,000
U.S. membership: 6 million
(1995 data from the American Muslim Council)

Canadian Islamic Centers and Organizations: 150
Canadian membership: 450,000
(1996 data from the Muslim World League)

MARRIAGE CEREMONY

Marriage is incumbent on every Muslim man and woman unless they are financially or physically unable to be married. It is regarded as the norm for all and essential to the growth and stability of the family, which is the basic unit of society. Marriage is regarded as a sacred contract or covenant, not a sacrament, that legalizes sexual intercourse and the procreation of children.

The marriage ceremony usually lasts about 30 minutes, but can last more than one hour. It is a ceremony in itself.

BEFORE THE CEREMONY

Are guests usually invited by a formal invitation?
Non-Muslims are usually invited orally, either over the telephone or in person. For Muslims, invitations may be posted in a mosque or announced after the noon prayers on Friday.

If not stated explicitly, should one assume that children are invited?
Yes.

If one can't attend, what should one do?
RSVP with regrets and send a gift, either money or whatever items one deems appropriate for the needs of the newlyweds.

APPROPRIATE ATTIRE

Men: Casual shirt and slacks. Head covering is not required.

Women: A dress or skirt and blouse are recommended. Clothing should cover the arms and hems should reach below the knees. A scarf is required to cover the head. Women may wear open-toed shoes and/or modest jewelry.

For both men and women, there are no rules regarding colors of clothing, but openly wearing crosses, Stars of David, jewelry with the signs of the zodiac and pendants with faces or heads of animals or people is discouraged.

GIFTS

Is a gift customarily expected?

Yes, either money or whatever items one deems appropriate for the needs of the newlyweds.

Should gifts be brought to the ceremony?

They can either be sent to the home of the newlyweds or brought to the ceremony.

THE CEREMONY

Where will the ceremony take place?

In a mosque.

When should guests arrive and where should they sit?

Arrive at the time called for the wedding to start. Sit wherever you wish.

If arriving late, are there times when a guest should *not* enter the ceremony?

No.

Are there times when a guest should *not* leave the ceremony?

No.

Who are the major officiants, leaders or participants at the ceremony and what do they do?

- *An imam*, or Islamic prayer leader, who usually delivers a sermon about marriage. This may be in Arabic if the newlyweds are Arabic-speaking or in English if they are English-speaking. Or it may be a mixture of both languages.
- *Two witnesses*, who witness the oral and written contract entered into by the bride and groom.
- *The groom*, who offers marriage to the bride.
- *The bride*, who accepts the offer.

What books are used?

None.

To indicate the order of the ceremony:

Weddings are brief and informal. There is no need to indicate the order of the event.

Will a guest who is not a Muslim be expected to do anything other than sit?
No.

Are there any parts of the ceremony in which a guest who is not a Muslim should *not* participate?
No.

If not disruptive to the ceremony, is it okay to:
▪ **Take pictures?** Yes.
▪ **Use a flash?** Yes.
▪ **Use a video camera?** Yes.
▪ **Use a tape recorder?** Yes.

(Note: Different Islamic centers have different policies regarding such matters as cameras and tape recorders. If you wish to use such equipment during the ceremony, check in advance with an official of the mosque or center.)

Will contributions to the mosque be collected at the ceremony?
There will not be a collection, but in some mosques, boxes are mounted on the wall for voluntary contributions. Non-Muslims are not expected to make a contribution since that would be perceived as having imposed an obligation upon guests and, thus, violate the traditional generosity shown toward guests in Islamic culture.

How much is customary to contribute?
This is entirely at the discretion of each person. Perhaps $1 to $5 maximum.

AFTER THE CEREMONY

Is there usually a reception after the ceremony?
Yes. This is called a *waleemah* ("wah-LEEH-mah"). It may last two hours or more and can be held anywhere: In the mosque, a home, a catering hall or any other site. Beverages and such food as meat, rice, fruit, and sweets will be served. There will be no alcoholic beverages. There may be dancing and/or music, but not if the *waleemah* is held in a mosque.

Would it be considered impolite to neither eat nor drink?
No.

Is there a grace or benediction before eating or drinking?
No.

Is there a grace or benediction after eating or drinking?

No.

Is there a traditional greeting for the family?

"*Mabrook alaik*" ("MAH-brook ah-LAYK"), "Congratulations," if addressing a male. "*Mabrook alaiki*" ("MAH-brook ah-LAYK-ee"), "Congratulations," if addressing a female.

Is there a traditional form of address for clergy who may be at the reception?

An imam may be directly addressed by the title of "imam" or by his name.

Is it okay to leave early?

Yes.

20

Jehovah's Witnesses

HISTORY AND BELIEFS

The Jehovah's Witnesses are a worldwide faith known for their assertive proselytizing and their expectations of an imminent apocalypse. They have drawn attention because of their refusal to celebrate Christmas, by their dedicated missionary work and by using Jehovah as the sole name of God.

Jehovah's Witnesses derive their name from the 43rd chapter of the Book of Isaiah, in which the gods of the nations are invited to bring forth their witnesses to prove their claimed cases of righteousness or to hear the witnesses for Jehovah's side and acknowledge the truth: "Ye are My witnesses, saith Jehovah, and My servants whom I have chosen; that ye may know and believe Me, and understand that I am He; before Me there was no God formed, neither shall there be after Me. I, even I, am Jehovah; and besides Me there is no savior" (Isaiah 43:10, 11, American Standard Version of the Bible).

In the Bible, all faithful worshippers, such as Abel, Noah, Abraham and Jesus, were called "witnesses of God" (Hebrews 11:1-12:1; Revelation 3:14).

The faith was founded in western Pennsylvania in the early 1870s by Charles Taze Russell, who had organized a Bible study group to promote the basic teachings of the Bible. It was his desire to return to the teachings of first-century Christianity.

Jehovah's Witnesses believe that God demands unconditional obedience and that the infallible source of truth is the Bible, which is true in every detail. Jesus, who was the Son of God and was His first creation, was responsible for all the rest of God's creation on earth. While residing on earth, Jesus was entirely a man. After His death, He was raised by God to heaven and restored to a place second only to that of His Father, Jehovah.

The fulfillment of God's kingdom will occur through the battle of Armageddon, the appearance of the Lord in the air, the thousand-year rule on earth of Christ (during which resurrection and judgment take place). This process began in 1914 and its completion will soon occur.

Members of the Church are expected to devote their primary loyalty and time to the movement, and not participate in politics or interfaith movements. They believe that all human laws that do not conflict with God's law should be obeyed. They also do not vote in civic elections or serve in the military. They respect each country's flag (or other national symbols), but do not salute it, since they believe this would be idolatry.

U.S. churches: 11,000
U.S. membership: 985,000

(*data from the* 1998 Yearbook of Jehovah's Witnesses)

Canadian churches: 1,400
Canadian membership: 114,000

(*data from the* 1998 Yearbook of Jehovah's Witnesses)

MARRIAGE CEREMONY

Jehovah's Witnesses view marriage as a sacred vow made before God. It seals a permanent union that can be broken only by infidelity or death.

The marriage ceremony, which may last about 30 minutes, is a ceremony in itself.

BEFORE THE CEREMONY

Are guests usually invited by a formal invitation?
Yes. An announcement is made in a Kingdom Hall issuing a general invitation to all members of the congregation. Guests who are not members of the congregation usually receive a written invitation.

If not stated explicitly, should one assume that children are invited?
Yes.

If one can't attend, what should one do?
Nothing is required if one is a member who has heard the invitation in a Kingdom Hall. If one has received a written invitation, RSVP with regrets.

APPROPRIATE ATTIRE

Men: A jacket and tie. No head covering is required.

Women: A dress or a skirt and blouse. Dress "modestly" and "sensibly." Hems need not reach below the knees nor must clothing cover the arms. Open-toed shoes and modest jewelry are permissible. No head covering is required.

There are no rules regarding colors of clothing.

GIFTS

Is a gift customarily expected?
While gifts are surely not required, they are certainly appropriate. Cash, bonds or such household items as sheets, kitchenware or small appliances are customary.

Should gifts be brought to the ceremony?
Either to the ceremony or to the reception afterward.

THE CEREMONY

Where will the ceremony take place?
In the main auditorium of a Kingdom Hall where Bible lectures are normally given.

When should guests arrive and where should they sit?
Arrive early to avoid causing a distraction. Attendants will seat guests. The front few rows are reserved for family.

If arriving late, are there times when a guest should *not* enter the ceremony?
No, but usually attendants will seat late-arriving guests in such a way as not to create a disturbance.

Are there times when a guest should *not* leave the ceremony?
No.

Who are the major officiants, leaders or participants at the ceremony and what do they do?
- *The Congregation Elder*, who gives a Bible talk to the bride and groom and solemnizes the marriage.
- *The bride and groom and their wedding party.*

What books are used?
The Old and New Testaments, primarily the New World Translation (New York: The Watchtower Bible and Tract Society of New York, 1961).

To indicate the order of the ceremony:
The officiating elder will make periodic announcements.

Will a guest who is not a Jehovah's Witness be expected to do anything other than sit?
No.

Are there any parts of the ceremony in which a guest who is not a Jehovah's Witness should *not* participate?
No.

If not disruptive to the ceremony, is it okay to:
◘ **Take pictures?** Yes.
◘ **Use a flash?** Yes.
◘ **Use a video camera?** Yes.
◘ **Use a tape recorder?** Yes.

(Note: Do not use the above equipment during prayer. Flash pictures should not be taken during the Bible talk since this can be very distracting.)

Will contributions to the church be collected at the ceremony?
No.

AFTER THE CEREMONY

Is there usually a reception after the ceremony?
Yes. It may be held in homes or a catering hall. It is never held in the Kingdom Hall where the wedding took place. Usually, refreshments are served. The reception may last more than two hours.

Would it be considered impolite to neither eat nor drink?
No.

Is there a grace or benediction before eating or drinking?
Yes.

Is there a grace or benediction after eating or drinking?
No.

Is there a traditional greeting for the family?
Just offer your congratulations.

Is there a traditional form of address for clergy who may be at the reception?
Either "Brother" or "Mr.," followed by last name.

Is it okay to leave early?
Yes.

21

Jewish

HISTORY AND BELIEFS

Judaism includes religious rituals and beliefs along with a code of ethical behavior. It also incorporates and reflects the ancient history of the Jews as a nation in its rituals, ceremonies and celebrations. Today, its adherents include people of every race and most nations.

The foundation of Judaism is the Torah, the first five books of the Bible (Genesis, Exodus, Leviticus, Numbers and Deuteronomy). According to the Torah, God made a covenant with the Jews, beginning with the three patriarchs: Abraham; his son, Isaac; and his grandson, Jacob, whose name God changed to "Israel." At a time when people worshipped many gods, the Jewish people, through this covenant, accepted the "One God" as the only God.

Central to this covenant is the concept of being "chosen" as a people, for as Moses tells his people in the Bible: "...The Lord has chosen you to be a people for His own possession, out of all the peoples that are on the face of the earth" (Deuteronomy 14:2). Being "chosen" does not confer special privilege. It means that the Jewish poeple are obliged to bring God's message to the world.

As part of God's covenant with Abraham, his descendants were promised the area now known as Israel—the Promised Land—as their homeland. They took possession of it in approximately 1200 B.C.E. (Before the Common Era, referred to as B.C. in the Christian calendar). In 70 C.E. (Common Era, referred to as A.D. in the Christian calendar), the conquering Romans destroyed Jerusalem and its Temple, which was the center of Jewish religious life, and drove the Jewish people from their land to end repeated rebellions. This began the period known as "The Diaspora," when the Jewish people were without a homeland. Many drifted to the northern and southern rim of the Mediterranean, while others emigrated eastward.

Jewish settlement in the American colonies began in 1654 in New Amsterdam (later called New York). Jewish immigration to Canada began in 1760, with the first synagogue being established in 1768. The modern Jewish state, Israel, was founded in 1948, three years after the end of the Holocaust in which six million Jews were killed.

Before the Diaspora, Judaism as a religion evolved under a hereditary priesthood that officiated at the Temple in Jerusalem, and through the ethical and moral teachings of a series of prophets. Following the Temple's destruction, religious leadership passed from priests to *rabbis*—teachers and scholars. Today, the rabbinate includes both men and women in all movements except the Orthodox.

There are now four major Jewish religious movements in the United States and Canada. In terms of theology, Reform Judaism is at the liberal end followed by Reconstructionist, Conservative, and Orthodox—both modern and traditional (which includes several fundamentalist groups, such as the Hasidim).

Hebrew, the traditional language of Jewish worship, is used to varying degrees in the services or celebrations of each movement. Each also has its own version of the prayerbook, and almost all include translations of the Hebrew material.

Reform Judaism, which began in the early 19th century in Germany, regards Judaism as an ongoing process resulting from the relationship between God and the Jewish people over its history. It considers Torah divinely inspired and subject to individual interpretation based on study, and emphasizes the ethical and moral messages of the prophets to help create a just society.

Reconstructionism, founded in the 1930s, is the most recent of the Jewish movements. Here the essence of Judaism is defined as embodying an entire civilization and not only a religion. At the core of this civilization is a people who have the authority and the responsibility to "reconstruct" its contents from generation to generation.

Conservative Judaism began in the mid-19th century as a reaction to what its founders perceived to be Reform's radicalism. It teaches that while the Torah as a whole is binding and that much of Jewish law remains authoritative, nonetheless new ideas and practices have always influenced Jewish beliefs and rituals and this should continue today, as well.

Orthodox Judaism teaches that Torah was divinely revealed to Moses at Mount Sinai and that the *halachah* ("hah-lah-KHAH"), the interpretative process of that law, is both divinely guided and authoritative. Thus, no law stemming from the Torah can be tampered with even if it displeases modern sensibilities. Orthodoxy often rejects more modern forms of Judaism as deviations from divine truths and authentic modes of Jewish life.

Houses of worship in the Orthodox, Conservative and Reconstructionist movement are typically called "synagogues." Usually, only a Reform house of worship is called a "temple."

U.S. synagogues/temples: Over 2,000 total
Reform: 890
Conservative: 800
Reconstructionist: 80
Orthodox: Not available

U.S. membership: 4.1 million total
Reform: 2 million
Conservative: 1.6 million
Reconstructionist: 100,000
Orthodox: 375,000 (estimate)

(1995 data from each denomination's central office, except Orthodox)

Canadian synagogues/temples: Over 248 total
Reform: 20
Conservative: 48
Reconstructionist: 2
Orthodox: 124

Canadian membership: Over 365,000 total
Reform: Not available
Conservative: Not available
Reconstructionist: Not available
Orthodox: Not available
(data from the Canadian Jewish Congress and the
1992 Corpus Almanac and Canadian Sourcebook)

MARRIAGE CEREMONY

Judaism considers marriage a divine command, a sacred bond and a means of personal fulfillment. Marriage is deemed the natural and desirable state of every adult. The Hebrew word for marriage is *kiddushin* ("kee-doo-SHEEN"), which means "sanctification."

The *huppah* ("hoo-PAH") or wedding canopy, under which the ceremony takes place, symbolizes the canopy of the heavens under which all life transpires. A glass, which the groom breaks underfoot after he and the bride have said their wedding vows, is an ancient tradition that has been interpreted in many ways, including commemorating at this time of great joy, a moment of great sadness: The destruction of the Temple in Jerusalem in 70 C.E. (Common Era).

The wedding ceremony is always a ceremony in itself. Not part of a larger service, it may take about 15 to 30 minutes.

BEFORE THE CEREMONY

Are guests usually invited by a formal invitation?
Yes.

If not stated explicitly, should one assume that children are invited?
No.

If one can't attend, what should one do?
RSVP with regrets and send a gift.

APPROPRIATE ATTIRE

Men: Attire depends on the social formality of the event. A small head covering called a *yarmulke* ("YAHR-mil-kah") or *kippah* ("keep-AH") is required in all Orthodox, Conservative and Reconstructionist ceremonies and in some Reform ceremonies. They will be provided to guests.

Women: Attire depends on the social formality of the event. For most Orthodox ceremonies, clothing, such as a dress or skirt and blouse, should be modest and cover the arms and hems should reach below the knees. Open-toed shoes and modest jewelry are appropriate. In some Orthodox and Conservative ceremonies, a head covering may be required.

Do not openly wear symbols of other faiths, such as a cross.

There are no rules regarding colors of clothing, but this is a very festive event.

GIFTS

Is a gift customarily expected?
Yes. Appropriate are such household items as small appliances or sheets or towels. Money is also appropriate, with amounts between $50 and $200 recommended. The bride often is listed in the bridal registry at a local department store.

Should gifts be brought to the ceremony?
No. Send them to the bride's home or to the reception.

THE CEREMONY

Where will the ceremony take place?
Depending on the desires of the couple, it may be at a synagogue/temple, a catering hall, at home or any other location chosen by them.

When should guests arrive and where should they sit?
It is customary to arrive at the time called. Ushers usually will be present to seat you. Otherwise, sit wherever you wish.

If arriving late, are there times when a guest should *not* enter the ceremony?
Do not enter during the processional or recessional.

Are there times when a guest should *not* leave the ceremony?
Not during the processional or recessional or while the officiant is blessing or addressing the couple.

Who are the major officiants, leaders or participants at the ceremony and what do they do?
- *The rabbi*, who leads the ceremony.
- *The cantor*, who sings during the ceremony or who may lead it instead of a rabbi.
- *The bride and groom.*
- *Parents of the bride and groom and other members of the wedding party.*

What books are used?
None. There may be special material prepared by the bridal couple.

To indicate the order of the ceremony:
There may be a program.

Will a guest who is not Jewish be expected to do anything other than sit?
No.

Are there any parts of the ceremony in which a guest who is not Jewish should *not* participate?
No.

If not disruptive to the ceremony, is it okay to:
- **Take pictures?** Possibly. Ask your host.
- **Use a flash?** Possibly. Ask your host.

⚄ Use a video camera? Possibly. Ask your host.
⚄ Use a tape recorder? Possibly. Ask your host.

Will contributions to the synagogue/temple be collected at the ceremony?
No.

AFTER THE CEREMONY

Is there usually a reception after the ceremony?
Weddings are times of great celebration. Often, a full meal is served at which there is music and dancing. This may be held in a reception room of the synagogue/temple, in a separate catering hall, at a hotel, or at another site. There may also be a light smorgasbord before the ceremony itself.

Guests should not expect to mix dairy and meat products at the reception if it is kosher (observes the traditional Jewish dietary laws). All Orthodox receptions, most Conservative and Reconstructionist and some Reform receptions are kosher.

Would it be considered impolite to neither eat nor drink?
No.

Is there a grace or benediction before eating or drinking?
Yes. Wait for a blessing to be said before eating or drinking. A benediction called *ha'motzi* ("hah-MOH-tsee") is recited before eating bread. It might be said by a rabbi, cantor or a lay person who is an honored guest.

Is there a grace or benediction after eating or drinking?
All Orthodox and many Conservative and Reconstructionist ceremonies have a grace after meals called *birkat hamazon*. This is increasingly common in Reform ceremonies.

Is there a traditional greeting for the family?
"Congratulations," or, in Hebrew, "*Mazal tov*" ("MAH-zal tohv").

Is there a traditional form of address for clergy who may be at the reception?
"Rabbi" or "cantor."

Is it okay to leave early?
Yes, but usually only after the main course has been served.

22

Lutheran

HISTORY AND BELIEFS

Lutherans trace their faith back to the German reformer, Martin Luther (1483-1546), who sought to reform doctrines and practices of the Roman Catholic Church. Objecting to the Church's teachings that one is saved by faith and by doing good works, he maintained that, according to the Bible, one is made just in God's eyes only by trusting in Jesus' accomplishments for humanity. This is distinct from any good that one does.

Luther also objected to corruption among the clergy and advocated worship in the language of the people rather than in Latin. He favored a married, rather than a celibate, clergy.

Although the Church of Rome considered Luther disloyal and drove him out, later, many priests and laity, especially in northern Germany, eventually agreed with Luther's teachings and revamped already existing churches around them.

German and Scandinavian immigrants brought the Lutheran faith to North America. By 1900, scores of small Lutheran church bodies were divided from one another by language, theology and the extent of their assimilation into North American society. Although still somewhat divided along ethnic lines, the main divisions today are between those who are theologically liberal and theologically conservative.

In the United States, the two main Lutheran denominations are the Evangelical Lutheran Church in America and the Lutheran Church–Missouri Synod. The former was created by uniting many earlier churches; the latter, which is a national Church despite its name, is more conservative theologically.

In Canada, the Evangelical Lutheran Church in Canada is comparable to the Evangelical Lutheran Church in America; while the Lutheran Church–Canada is the Canadian counterpart to the Lutheran Church–Missouri Synod, and relates closely to that body.

The Evangelical Lutheran Church in America:
U.S. churches: 11,000
U.S. membership: 5.2 million

The Lutheran Church–Missouri Synod:
U.S. churches: 6,100
U.S. membership: 2.6 million

(*data from the* 1998 Yearbook of American and Canadian Churches)

The Evangelical Lutheran Church in Canada:
Canadian churches: 864
Canadian membership: 198,683

Lutheran Church–Canada:
Canadian churches: 387
Canadian membership: 84,763
(*data from* Directory, Lutheran Churches in Canada, *1997)*

MARRIAGE CEREMONY

For Lutherans, a church wedding is an act of worship, not a civil service. In the service, the couple profess their love for and their commitment to each other before God and ask His blessing on their marriage. The same decorum exercised in any worship service should be exercised in the wedding service.

The ceremony may either be a service unto itself or be part of the Holy Communion service. The bridal party will proceed in, then the pastor will read appropriate lessons from the Bible and ask the bride and groom about their lifelong commitment to one another. The pastor will deliver a brief homily, wedding vows and rings will be exchanged, and the pastor will pronounce the couple husband and wife.

If the ceremony is a service by itself, it will last 15 to 30 minutes. If part of the celebration of Holy Communion and also depending on the music selected, it will last around half an hour.

BEFORE THE CEREMONY

Are guests usually invited by a formal invitation?
Yes.

If not stated explicitly, should one assume that children are invited?
Yes.

If one can't attend, what should one do?
Reply in writing or call and send a gift.

APPROPRIATE ATTIRE

Local social norms prevail, although weddings tend to be somewhat formal.

Men: Jacket and tie. No head covering required.

Women: Dress, skirt and blouse, or pants suit are acceptable. Open-toed shoes and modest jewelry are fine. Hems need not reach the knees. No head covering required.

There are no rules regarding colors of clothing.

GIFTS

Is a gift customarily expected?
Yes. Appropriate gifts are such household items as appliances, dishes, towels or blankets. The bride often is listed in the bridal registry at a local department store.

Should gifts be brought to the ceremony?
If you are also invited to the reception afterwards, gifts are more often brought to the reception and placed on the gift table there.

THE CEREMONY

Where will the ceremony take place?
In the main sanctuary of the House of Worship. The bridal party will stand near the altar in the chancel, the area in front of the sanctuary which includes the altar and pulpit and seating for clergy.

When should guests arrive and where should they sit?
It is appropriate to arrive before the time called for the ceremony. An usher will tell you where to sit.

If arriving late, are there times when a guest should *not* enter the ceremony?
Do not enter during the processional, recessional or during prayer.

Are there times when a guest should *not* leave the ceremony?
Do not leave during the processional, recessional or during prayer.

Who are the major officiants, leaders or participants at the ceremony and what do they do?

◾ *The pastor,* who presides.
◾ *The bride and groom and their wedding party.*

What books are used?

A hymnal may be used.

To indicate the order of the ceremony:

There will be a program.

Will a guest who is not a Lutheran be expected to do anything other than sit?

Guests are not expected to do anything other than sit and enjoy.

Are there any parts of the ceremony in which a guest who is not a Lutheran should *not* participate?

Who is welcome to receive Holy Communion varies among Lutheran churches. The worship bulletin will usually state the policy for visitors.

If not disruptive to the ceremony, is it okay to:

◾ **Take pictures?** Only with prior permission from the pastor.
◾ **Use a flash?** Only with prior permission from the pastor.
◾ **Use a video camera?** Only with prior permission from the pastor.
◾ **Use a tape recorder?** Only with prior permission from the pastor.

Will contributions to the church be collected at the ceremony?

No.

AFTER THE CEREMONY

Is there usually a reception after the ceremony?

Customs vary locally and by individual preference. However, there will generally be a reception in the church, at home or in a catering hall. Depending on local custom, there may be music and dancing. The menu will vary from light refreshments and cake to a full meal. Alcoholic beverages may be served if the reception is held outside the church.

If the reception is held at a church, it will be less than 30 minutes. If at a home or restaurant, it will usually last at least two hours.

Would it be considered impolite to neither eat nor drink?

Yes. If you have dietary restrictions, inform your host or hostess in advance.

Is there a grace or benediction before eating or drinking?
Guests should wait for the saying of grace or an invocation before eating.

Is there a grace or benediction after eating or drinking?
No.

Is there a traditional greeting for the family?
Congratulate the new couple and their parents.

Is there a traditional form of address for clergy who may be at the reception?
"Pastor" followed by last name.

Is it okay to leave early?
Yes.

23

Mennonite/Amish

HISTORY AND BELIEFS

There are nearly 20 organized groups of Mennonites in North America. They vary in life style and religious practice, but all originate from the same sixteenth century Anabaptist movement in Europe. The Anabaptist movement began when a small group of religious reformers claimed Protestant reformers were not sufficiently "radical." They also differed with mainstream Protestants on the timing of baptism. Protestants called for baptism of infants, while Anabaptists mandated that one should be baptized after reaching an "age of accountability," which usually begins with early adolescence and confers the ability to profess belief for one's self.

The name "Mennonite" is derived from that of the sixteenth century Dutch Anabaptist leader, Menno Simons. Originally a Roman Catholic priest, Simons became convinced of the falsity of traditional Catholic doctrine and practice of his time, but hesitated at breaking with the Church. He joined the Anabaptists, who were then being persecuted. Grateful for his leadership, the group later adopted a variation on his name.

Over the years, Mennonites have maintained cultural traditions and religious beliefs in differing ways. While this has led to the formation of various Mennonite groups, they hold certain beliefs in common. Among these are that one should emulate Jesus in everyday living and behavior; that the Bible is the inspired word of God; and that Jesus taught the way of peace. Mennonite faith cannot easily be labeled a liberal or a conservative Christian denomination. Rather, it is an alternative to mainstream religion, one that emphasizes evangelism, peace and justice, and that focuses on a holistic approach to Christ's way of personal salvation, while maintaining concern for the physical as well as the spiritual needs of others.

The one over-arching Mennonite belief that differs from all Christian denominations (except for the Society of Friends, or "Quakers," and the Church of the Brethren) is the Church's stand on war and violence. In principle, Mennonites have always been conscientious objectors to war, although individual members have opted for non-combatant roles and even military service. More recently, the broadest emphasis has been placed on "non-violence" so it includes such issues as abortion and capital punishment.

Mennonites began emigrating to North America from Switzerland in the mid-seventeenth century, spreading westward from Pennsylvania and concentrating on rural colonies where they practiced their faith and Swiss culture.

In a second spurt of Mennonite emigration in the late nineteenth century, Mennonites of Dutch, German and Swiss ancestry who had settled in the Ukraine fled Czarist efforts to conscript them into the Russian army. They settled primarily in the Midwestern areas of the United States and Canada. A third and fourth wave of emigration followed both world wars.

An emphasis on missionary work in this century has helped the Church develop so much into an international institution that now more than one-third of adult Mennonites are non-whites. Mennonites combine a keen sense of evangelism with a theology of relief and material aid to people in want. For 75 years, the Mennonite Central Committee, a relief agency operating around the world, has helped the needy and addressed issues of peace and justice.

The Amish, or the Amish-Mennonite, as they are more properly known, originated from a disagreement among European Mennonites regarding "shunning," a practice that had been adopted by the Dutch Mennonites in 1632. Shunning demanded avoiding a fellow Mennonite who had transgressed. In the late 17th century, a Swiss Mennonite, Jacob Ammann, became concerned over laxity in the Swiss and Alsatian Mennonite communities when a woman who had admitted speaking a falsehood was not shunned. Ammann also rejected a prevalent belief that the souls would be saved of those who were sincerely sympathetic to the Mennonite, but did not join the faith. And he urged simplicity and uniformity as a guard against pride. This included the admonition that men not trim their beards. Today, the Amish call for simplicity extends to not using motorized vehicles, partly because of concerns that they could take Amish too far from their own community.

The group that eventually coalesced around Ammann and his teachings called themselves "Amish" in his honor. The first Amish arrived in North America around 1727, but a congregation was not formed until 1749 in Berks County, Pennsylvania. By the mid-19th century, there were significant Amish communities in Lancaster and Chester counties in Pennsylvania and in Holmes County, Ohio, as well as in Waterloo County, Ontario, Canada.

The largest Mennonite and Amish denominations in the United States are the Mennonite Church, with 1,004 churches and almost 91,000 members; the Old Order Amish Church, which is widely known for its resistance to modern technology, with 898 churches and almost 81,000 members; and the General Conference Mennonite Church, with 270 churches and 36,685 members.

Smaller, more traditional denominations include the Beachy Amish Mennonite (138 churches; 8,399 members); the Fellowship of Evangelical Bible Churches (37 churches; 4,039 members); and the Reformed Mennonite Church (10 churches; 346 members).

The largest Mennonite and Amish denominations in Canada include the Conference of Mennonites in Canada–General Conference, Mennonite Church, with 223 churches and 33,123 members (including 8,145 members from the Mennonite Church); the General Conference of the Mennonite Brethren Churches–Canada, with 207 churches and 28,368 members; and various Russian Mennonite immigrant groups numbering 20,164 members.

Smaller, more traditional denominations include Old Order Mennonite (5,763 members); Beachy Amish and Old Order Amish (1,612 members); Mennonite Church (independent and unaffiliated groups, 2,187 members).

U.S. churches: 2,455
U.S. membership: 266,693
(*data from the* 1998 Yearbook of American and Canadian Churches)

Canadian churches: 3,126
Canadian membership: 91,217
(*data compiled from* Mennonite World Conference Directory, 1994; Mennonite Year Book, 1997; *and* 1998 Yearbook of American and Canadian Churches)

MARRIAGE CEREMONY

Mennonites and Amish believe that marriage was instituted by God for companionship, procreation and the nurturing of children. Those who marry should share a common Christian commitment. Divorce constitutes a basic violation of God's will.

A Mennonite or Amish wedding is an act of worship in which the couple profess their love for and their commitment to each other before God and ask His blessing on their wedding. The same decorum exercised in any worship service should be exercised in the wedding service.

During the ceremony, the wedding party progresses in, then the pastor reads appropriate lessons from the Bible and asks the bride and groom about their commitment to one another. The pastor delivers a brief homily, weddings vows and rings are exchanged, and the couple are pronounced man and wife.

The wedding is often a ceremony in itself but may be part of a larger worship service. It usually lasts about 30 to 60 minutes, although some may last more than one hour.

BEFORE THE CEREMONY

Are guests usually invited by a formal invitation?

Yes.

If not stated explicitly, should one assume that children are invited?

No.

If one can't attend, what should one do?

RSVP with regrets and send a gift. (Note: Gifts are not expected at weddings of the General Conference of Mennonite Brethren.)

APPROPRIATE ATTIRE

Men: In more conservative denominations, such as the Beachy Amish Mennonite, a suit jacket coat is worn, but without a tie. In other denominations, such as the General Conference Mennonite Church or the General Conference of Mennonite Brethren, a jacket and tie are worn. No head covering is required.

Women: In more conservative denominations, such as the Beachy Amish Mennonite, women are expected to wear dresses that cover their arms and have hems that reach below their knees. Neither open-toed shoes nor modest jewelry are permissible. Church members cover their heads, but visitors are not expected to do so.

In less conservative denominations, such as the General Conference Mennonite Church or the General Conference of Mennonite Brethren, women may wear a dress or a skirt and blouse. Clothing need not cover women's arms nor hems reach below the knees. Open-toed shoes and modest jewelry are permissible. No head covering is required.

Dark, solid colors are advised for more conservative denominations, such as the Beachy Amish Mennonite. For less conservative denominations, there are no rules regarding colors of clothing.

GIFTS

Is a gift customarily expected?

Gifts are not expected at weddings in the General Conference of Mennonite Brethren. They are generally expected at weddings of other Mennonite denominations. Items for setting up a household are appropriate.

Should gifts be brought to the ceremony?

Yes.

THE CEREMONY

Where will the ceremony take place?

In the main sanctuary of the church.

When should guests arrive and where should they sit?

Arrive shortly before the time for which the ceremony has been called. Ushers will advise guests where to sit.

If arriving late, are there times when a guest should *not* enter the ceremony?

Do not enter during the procession of the wedding party or while prayers are being recited.

Are there times when a guest should *not* leave the ceremony?

No.

Who are the major officiants, leaders or participants at the ceremony and what do they do?

- *The bishop or pastor* (depending on the denomination) who performs the wedding ceremony.
- *The bride and groom and their parents.*
- *Musicians and/or song leaders.*

What books are used?

In each denomination, various translations of the Bible are used. In the Mennonite Brethren Church, the most common versions are the New International Version and the New Revised Standard Version. More conservative denominations may use the King James Version.

Various hymnals are also used throughout the denominations. The Mennonite Church and the General Conference Mennonite Church use *Hymnal: A Worship Book* (Newton, Kans.: Faith and Life Press, 1992). The Mennonite Brethren Church uses *Worship Together* (Fresno, Calif.: The Board of Faith and Life, The General Conference of Mennonite Brethren Churches, 1995).

To indicate the order of the ceremony:

A program will be distributed.

Will a guest who is neither Mennonite nor Amish be expected to do anything other than sit?

Guests are expected to stand with congregants when they arise. If it does not violate their religious beliefs, it is optional for them to sing and read prayers aloud with the congregants.

Are there any parts of the ceremony in which a guest who is neither Mennonite nor Amish should *not* participate?

If the wedding is part of a broader worship service at which communion is offered, it is not given to guests who are not Christian.

If not disruptive to the ceremony, is it okay to:

- **Take pictures?** Not allowed in most denominations. Possibly (and only with prior permission of the pastor) in the General Conference of Mennonite Brethren.
- **Use a flash?** Not allowed in most denominations. Possibly (and only with prior permission of the pastor) in the General Conference of Mennonite Brethren.
- **Use a video camera?** Not allowed in most denominations. Possibly (and only with prior permission of the pastor) in the General Conference of Mennonite Brethren.
- **Use a tape recorder?** Not allowed in most denominations. Possibly (and only with prior permission of the pastor) in the General Conference of Mennonite Brethren.

Will contributions to the church be collected at the ceremony?

No.

AFTER THE CEREMONY

Is there usually a reception after the ceremony?

Yes. This is usually held in the same building as the wedding ceremony. Refreshments may range from sandwiches, nuts and beverages to a full meal. Almost always, cake and ice cream are served. There will be no alcoholic beverages. There will be no dancing, although musicians may play background music after weddings of some less conservative denominations (such as the General Conference Mennonite Church). The reception may last from 30 minutes to more than two hours.

Would it be considered impolite to neither eat nor drink?

No.

Is there a grace or benediction before eating or drinking?

Possibly.

Is there a grace or benediction after eating or drinking?

No.

Is there a traditional greeting for the family?

"Congratulations" or "Best wishes."

Is there a traditional form of address for clergy who may be at the reception?

"Pastor."

Is it okay to leave early?

Yes.

24

Methodist

HISTORY AND BELIEFS

The Methodist movement began in 18th-century England under the preaching of John Wesley, an Anglican priest who was a prodigious evangelical preacher, writer and organizer. While a student at Oxford University, he and his brother, Charles, led the Holy Club of devout students, whom scoffers called the "Methodists."

Wesley's teachings affirmed the freedom of human will as promoted by grace. He saw each person's depth of sin matched by the height of sanctification to which the Holy Spirit, the empowering spirit of God, can lead persons of faith.

Although Wesley remained an Anglican and disavowed attempts to form a new church, Methodism eventually became another church body. During a conference in Baltimore, Maryland, in 1784, the Methodist Church was founded as an ecclesiastical organization and the first Methodist bishop in the United States was elected.

The Methodist movement was first represented in Canada by Laurence Coughlan, who began to preach in Newfoundland in 1766. It wasn't until 1884, however, that the Methodist Church was formed in Canada from the merger of the Methodist Episcopal Church and smaller Methodist bodies, with the Wesleyan Methodist Church, the Conference of Eastern British America and the New Connexion Church, which had united in 1874. The Free Methodists, entering from the U.S. in 1876, were few in number and have remained separate.

In the nineteenth century, strong missionary programs helped plant Methodism abroad. Methodist missionaries from America followed their

British colleagues to India and Africa, where they founded new churches. Americans and Canadians also founded churches in East Asia, Latin America and continental Europe.

Local Methodist churches are called "charges." Their ministers are appointed by the bishop at an annual conference, and each church elects its own administrative board, which initiates planning and sets local goals and policies.

There are about 125 Methodist denominations around the globe and 23 separate Methodist bodies in the United States. Of these, the United Methodist Church is numerically the largest.

In Canada, the Methodist Church ceased to exist as a separate denomination in 1925, when it joined with Congregationalists and the majority of Presbyterian churches to form the United Church of Canada. The Free Methodist Church in Canada, which was incorporated in 1927 and which gained full autonomy from the U.S. parent denomination in 1990, remains intact.

U.S. churches: 36,361
U.S. membership: 8.5 million
(*data from the* 1998 Yearbook of American and Canadian Churches)

Canadian churches: 129
Canadian membership: 5,360
(*data from the* 1998 Yearbook of American and Canadian Churches)

MARRIAGE CEREMONY

Methodist denominations affirm that marriage is the uniting of a man and a woman in a union that is intended—and which is pledged—to be lifelong.

The marriage ceremony is a service in itself. It may last between 15 and 30 minutes.

BEFORE THE CEREMONY

Are guests usually invited by a formal invitation?
Yes.

If not stated explicitly, should one assume that children are invited?
No.

If one can't attend, what should one do?
RSVP with your regrets and send a gift.

APPROPRIATE ATTIRE

Men: Jacket and tie. No head covering is required.

Women: A dress. The arms do not necessarily have to be covered nor do hems have to be below the knees. Open-toed shoes and modest jewelry are permissible. No head covering is required.

There are no rules regarding colors of clothing.

GIFTS

Is a gift ordinarily expected?
Yes. Such gifts as small appliances, sheets, towels or other household gifts are appropriate.

Should gifts be brought to the ceremony?
No, send them to the home of the newlyweds.

THE CEREMONY

Where will the ceremony take place?
Usually in the main sanctuary of a church.

When should guests arrive and where should they sit?
Arrive early. Depending on the setting, ushers may show guests where to sit.

If arriving late, are there times when a guest should *not* enter the ceremony?
Ushers will assist latecomers.

Are there times when a guest should *not* leave the ceremony?
No.

Who are the major officiants, leaders or participants at the ceremony and what do they do?
- *The pastor,* who officiates.
- *The bride and groom.*
- *The wedding party.*

What books are used?
Possibly a hymnal.

To indicate the order of the ceremony:
A program will be provided.

Will a guest who is not a Methodist be expected to do anything other than sit?

Standing and kneeling with the congregation and reading prayers aloud and singing with congregants are all optional. Guests are welcome to participate if this does not compromise their personal beliefs.

Are there any parts of the ceremony in which a guest who is not a Methodist should *not* participate?

Yes. Holy Communion may be offered at the service. Methodists invite all to receive Holy Communion, but guests should be aware that partaking of communion is regarded as an act of identification with Christianity. Feel free to remain seated as others go forward for communion. Likewise, if communion bread and cups are passed among the pews, feel free to pass them along without partaking.

If not disruptive to the ceremony, is it okay to:
◗ **Take pictures?** Possibly. Ask ushers.
◗ **Use a flash?** Possibly. Ask ushers.
◗ **Use a video camera?** Possibly. Ask ushers.
◗ **Use a tape recorder?** Possibly. Ask ushers.

Will contributions to the church be collected at the ceremony?
No.

AFTER THE CEREMONY

Is there usually a reception after the ceremony?
There is often a reception that may last one to two hours. It may be at a home, a catering facility or in the same building as the ceremony. Ordinarily, food and beverages are served and there is dancing and music. Alcoholic beverages may be served.

Would it be considered impolite to neither eat nor drink?
No.

Is there a grace or benediction before eating or drinking?
No.

Is there a grace or benediction after eating or drinking?
No.

Is there a traditional greeting for the family?
No. Just offer your congratulations.

Is there a traditional form of address for clergy who may be at the reception?

"Reverend" or "Pastor."

Is it okay to leave early?

Yes, but usually only after toasts have been made and the wedding cake has been served.

25

Mormon (Church of Jesus Christ of Latter-day Saints)

HISTORY AND BELIEFS

The Church of Jesus Christ of Latter-day Saints, the largest indigenous American religious group, was founded by Joseph Smith in the early 19th century. Living in upstate New York, Smith had a vision in 1820 in which God and Jesus Christ appeared to him. Three years later, the angel Moroni told him of the location of gold tablets containing God's revelations. In 1830, Smith published a translation of these revelations entitled *The Book of Mormon*. He soon became the "seer, translator, prophet and apostle" of a group committed to restoring the church established centuries before by Christ.

Latter-day Saints stressed the coming of Christ's Kingdom to earth and encouraged others to adhere to the teachings of the Savior.

Smith's group moved first to Ohio, and then to Missouri, where violence ensued prompted by their polygamy and their anti-slavery stance. Persecution forced the group to move to Illinois, where they built their own city and named it Nauvoo. In 1844, while imprisoned for destroying an opposition printing press, Smith was killed by a mob that attacked the jail.

Schisms erupted amid the subsequent leadership vacuum and concern over polygamy, a practice that Smith had said in 1843 had come to him in a vision and which became Church doctrine in 1852. Most Latter-day Saints followed the leadership of Brigham Young, who led them into the Great Salt Lake area of what is now Utah. Latter-day Saints are headquartered there to this day.

While many Latter-day Saints' beliefs are similar to orthodox Christian ideas, Smith uniquely taught that God, although omniscient, has a material body. He taught that through repentance and baptism by immersion, anyone can gain entrance to Christ's earthly kingdom. Through "proxies" who receive baptism in a Latter-day Saints' temple, the dead may also share in the highest of post-mortal rewards or blessings.

The Church teaches that men and women are equal in the eyes of the Lord and that they cannot achieve the highest eternal rewards without each other.

The charge given by Jesus to Matthew, "Go ye unto all the world" to share the teachings of His gospel, motivates the Church's 57,000 full-time missionaries around the world. Most are college-age males who serve for two years at their own expense. Their success has led to the church currently having more than 25,000 congregations in 160 nations and territories around the world.

In addition to churches, where worship services are conducted, temples are located around the world. These are closed on Sundays, but open every other day of the week for marriages and other sacred ordinances. Only faithful members of the Church may enter a temple.

U.S. churches and temples: 10,000+
U.S. membership: 4.3 million
(1995 data from The Church of Jesus Christ of Latter-day Saints)

Canadian churches and temples: 450+
Canadian membership: 150,000
(1997 data from The Church of Jesus Christ of Latter-day Saints)

MARRIAGE CEREMONY

Reflecting the Church's emphasis on strong family solidarity and the potential for eternal family relationships, Latter-day Saints believe that marriage performed in a Church temple need not end at death, but, instead, has the potential of continuing forever. Also reflecting Church interpretations of the "strict morality" taught by Jesus are proscriptions against adultery and prescriptions for absolute fidelity during marriage.

BEFORE THE CEREMONY

Are guests usually invited by a formal invitation?
Yes.

If not stated explicitly, should one assume that children are invited?
Children do not attend a marriage ceremony performed in the temples, but they may be invited to a ceremony performed in a church or a civil ceremony performed elsewhere.

If one can't attend, what should one do?
RSVP with regrets.

APPROPRIATE ATTIRE

Men: A suit or sport jacket and tie. No head covering required.

Women: A dress or a skirt and blouse. No head covering required, but the overall fashion statement should be conservative and dignified. Hems should be near the knees. Open-toed shoes and modest jewelry are permissible.

Modest and dignified clothing is appreciated.

GIFTS

Is a gift customarily expected?
The option to present a gift (and the nature of the gift) is left to the invited individual.

Should gifts be brought to the ceremony?
Gifts are traditionally presented at postnuptial receptions.

THE CEREMONY

Where will the ceremony take place?
Members of the Church are encouraged to be married in one of its temples, which are located around the world. A temple, which is different from a local church building where worship services are conducted, is closed on Sundays, but open every other day of the week for marriages and other sacred ordinances.

Only faithful members of the Church may enter a temple. Guests invited to the temple marriage ceremony must present a "temple recommend" issued by their bishop to indicate that they are, indeed, faithful members.

A couple may also choose to be married in a local church meetinghouse, a home or another location.

When should guests arrive and where should they sit?
Arrive at the time for which the service is called and sit wherever you wish.

If arriving late, are there times when a guest should *not* enter the ceremony?
No.

Are there times when a guest should *not* leave the ceremony?
Leaving early is discouraged.

Who are the major officiants, leaders or participants at the ceremony and what do they do?
Authorized clergy perform the ceremony.

What books are used?
Possibly Scriptures.

Will a guest who is not a Latter-day Saint be expected to do anything other than sit?
No.

Are there any parts of the ceremony in which a guest who is not a Latter-day Saint should *not* participate?
All guests only observe the ceremony.

If not disruptive to the ceremony, is it okay to:
◤ **Take pictures?** No.
◤ **Use a flash?** No.
◤ **Use a video camera?** No.
◤ **Use a tape recorder?** No.

Will contributions to the church be collected at the ceremony?
No.

AFTER THE CEREMONY

Is there usually a reception after the ceremony?
There is usually a reception, but where it is held and what is done there is the personal choice of the bride and groom. Traditionally, it is an open-house type of affair.

Would it be considered impolite to neither eat nor drink?
No.

Is there a grace or benediction before eating or drinking?
Possibly. This is the choice of the hosts.

Is there a grace or benediction after eating or drinking?
No.

Is there a traditional greeting for the family?

No. Just offer your congratulations.

Is there a traditional form of address for clergy who may be at the reception?

A bishop is referred to as "Bishop," followed by his last name. His counselors are addressed as "Brother," followed by their last names.

Is it okay to leave early?

Yes, since at the traditional open-house type of reception guests stay as long as they feel is appropriate.

26

Native American/First Nations

Native American/First Nations religion does not exist as a single, readily identifiable faith. (In practice, few Native Peoples use the word "religion" to describe their traditional ceremonies and practices. The term is used here to help those outside the community relate in some way to the understandings and "the way of life" of aboriginal/indigenous peoples.) Indigenous Americans (whom United States law recognizes as American Indians and Alaska Natives) and First Nations peoples in Canada have diverse and rich religious traditions. Although it is impossible to generalize about the diverse ceremonial practices of Native Americans/First Nations peoples, some suggestions regarding respectful behavior at their religious ceremonies can be made based on the beliefs and values that are the foundation of their deeply spiritual worldviews.

Because these beliefs and values are intimately related to Native people's sense of the sacred, they directly influence what would count as respectful and appropriate behavior for those invited to attend most Native American/First Nations religious ceremonies. Since even those who are well-intentioned are often not aware of these beliefs and values, they may behave in ways that Native Peoples interpret as disrespectful toward their religious ceremonies and practices. Diverse religious traditions explain why those who have briefly visited—or actually lived—with Native Peoples report that they have encountered a people who are deeply connected to the sacred.

According to the 1990 United States census, American Indian and Alaska Native population totals approximately 1.9 million. Although this is roughly one percent of the total population of the United States, the more than 500 nations of the Native Peoples represent approximately 90 percent of the ethnic diversity in the United States. Among Native Peoples, there are nine major language families with almost 200 distinct dialects. From a constitutional viewpoint, the First Americans are citizens of their own various nations as well as of the United States.

Many First Nations people in Canada do not consider themselves to be "American" nor, for that matter, citizens of Canada. They see themselves as people of First Nations communities such as "Whata First Nations," or "Shawanaga First Nations," or "Peepeekisis First Nations." "Indian" is a term specifically used by the government of Canada to define certain aboriginal people mentioned in the Indian Act of 1867 and excludes many people of aboriginal ancestry. There are 53 aboriginal languages in Canada, including Inuit and Metis languages.

If you consider the geographic and cultural diversity of the five largest tribal groups in the United States alone—the Cherokee in North Carolina and Oklahoma, the Navajo in Arizona and New Mexico, the Chippewa of the Northern and Great Lakes regions, the Sioux (which include the Lakota, Dakota and Nakota) spread across the Northern Plains, and the Choctaw in Mississippi and Oklahoma—you begin to grasp why it is impossible to generalize about the cultural practices, and specifically the religious ceremonies and practices, of Native American/First Nations peoples.

HISTORY AND BELIEFS

Over the last 500 years, Native Peoples have endured what they consider to be almost constant disrespect. Recognizing this unpleasant legacy will help those desiring to visit Native American religious ceremonies understand why many Native Peoples are wary about sharing the most important elements of their identity with those who do not share their faith.

In 1879, for instance, the Carlisle Indian Boarding School was created in Carlisle, Pennsylvania. This was the first of what would eventually be dozens of off-reservation boarding schools designed to "solve" the "Indian Problem." In the late 1870s, the federal government assumed that the "Indian Problem" could be eradicated by education built around creating institutions dedicated to the complete cultural assimilation of First American boys and girls and erasing their beliefs, values and culture. Similar policies were enacted by the federal government of Canada.

Not surprisingly, given the centrality of the sacred to Native culture and identity, completely eradicating their indigenous religious and spiritual traditions was deemed a prerequisite for successful "education." Christian clergy often ran these schools since "civilizing" these children meant converting them to Christianity.

Understanding just this small part of the history of Native Peoples when attending their religious events and ceremonies can help you appreciate the intrinsically communitarian and private nature of their religious practices.

Native American/First Nations religion is primarily about experience, not about theology or doctrine.

It is simultaneously a personal and a profoundly communal experience. The nearly universal rule among Native Peoples that explains this is that ceremonies, customs and various cultural traditions, which are all ways of exercising spirituality, are, at their core, *community* activities for community members. Religious experience is profoundly shaped by one's membership and involvement in a community and one's life at a specific geographic place in relation to the whole of Creation.

Native spirituality denies the dichotomies common to Western religions.

The Western dualisms of supernatural vs. natural, spiritual vs. earthly/worldly, sacred vs. profane and heaven vs. hell do not easily fit with Native spirituality. Unlike religious traditions that see life on earth filled primarily with evil, toil and suffering, Native spirituality perceives the world as deeply endowed with the sacred power of the Creator.

Native languages, oral traditions, symbols, ceremonial objects and ceremonial practices speak directly to the recognition that humans are surrounded by the spiritual power of the Creator. Traditional prayers and ceremonies embody the widely held belief that we are imbued with one small part of the spirit of our Creator.

For Native peoples, the entire natural world is full of the sacred.

Each living part of Creation, and especially the places important to each tribe or village, serve as but one entrance into the power of the sacred. With this recognition of the complexity of Creation and the Creator's power comes the obvious realization that humans are but one part of the natural world, and not necessarily a privileged part or even the only "persons" inhabiting the earth.

Consequently, the high degree of religious diversity among Native Peoples reflects another widely shared element in traditional Native religious practices.

Native religious activities are almost universally attached to specific places.

These sacred sites mark the appropriate place for the enactment of certain ceremonies and religious activities. Even Native Peoples who experienced painful removal and relocation from their indigenous homelands in the eighteenth and nineteenth centuries found sacred sites in places new to them where their religious traditions could be carried out.

Most Native sacred sites are not analogous to a church, a temple or a shrine, which are consecrated as sacred by humans and built from blueprints, plans and drawings. Instead, Native ceremonial sites are often located on the land where specific tribes identify their spiritual center.

The places Native Peoples identify as their respective homelands and the communities that exist there are at the center of their religious experience. At the most fundamental level, the rich spirituality of Native peoples is literally "grounded" in their experience of the natural world as the cathedral of their Creator.

Native religious traditions are profoundly holistic.

Native faiths or teachings often refer to Creation itself as a complex web of life or a sacred circle in which all aspects of the natural world connect to each other. Because of this, humanity, in most Native worldviews, does not hold a privileged place above the rest of Creation, but is understood to be only a small part of Creation.

In many Native worldviews, many "persons" other than humans inhabit the world. Native Peoples attribute the qualities of power, consciousness and volition generally identified with the Western view of personhood to many living things. Consequently, Native Peoples perceive the environment to be inhabited with four-legged "persons" that swim in the water or winged "persons" that fly. To the Native way of thinking, these "persons" are also part of the moral and political community. Most importantly, they are also part of the spiritual community. In Native thought, to recognize that the earth is sacred is also to acknowledge all the "members" of our many respective communities.

The holistic nature of Native worldviews and spirituality gives a centrality to the idea of balance in one's life and in the world. Living in a good, healthy, beautiful way requires one to recognize that growth and success are achieved by integrating psychological, physical and spiritual well-being.

Native religious traditions openly acknowledge the existence of unseen powers.

Forces and mysteries exist that First Peoples experience and recognize, but cannot see or fully understand or comprehend. These sacred powers are not mysteries that need to be solved, but exist because humanity cannot know and understand everything about Creation or the Creator.

Native religions have no tradition of proselytizing.

Spiritual leaders and wisdom keepers do not undertake missionary activities. Their dependence on experience and on understanding the diversity of the circle of life makes it perfectly acceptable—and, perhaps to them, inevitable—that people from different places will have different religions. Consequently, First Peoples were always confused by other people who insisted they be just like them. This appreciation for the biological and cultural diversity of Mother Earth and her children explains Native respect for people's different ways of honoring the Creator and Creation. It also explains why Native people are often wary of those so interested in their traditions when the Creator gave all human beings a knowledge of the sacred.

MARRIAGE CEREMONIES

In Native American/First Nation belief, one of the central functions of the marriage ceremony is to impress upon the participants (in this case, the bride and groom) the importance of the new stage of life they are entering. The marriage ceremony both celebrates the event and prepares the new husband and wife to begin their journey together in a good way.

Traditionally, marriage ceremonies have always been community celebrations, although they have also been modernized in some ways. As Nico Strange Owl-Raben explained in an article about her Cheyenne wedding in a 1991 issue of *Native Peoples* magazine,

> I use the word "tradition" carefully. Tradition is not a stagnant thing. It is always changing and adapting. My wedding could not have been like my grandmother's. It was not possible. I have heard about the changes in my grandmother's generation and I have seen what happened in my mother's. Now my generation is experiencing change. My wedding incorporated tradition so that we could have a blend.

Consequently, contemporary Native wedding ceremonies often combine old and new ways. For instance, Ms. Strange Owl-Raben's Cheyenne wedding combined traditional Cheyenne attire, custom and symbolism with some modern societal conventions. The ceremony was held outside amid a semi-circle of tipis that had been erected in a Northern Rocky Mountain alpine meadow—a cathedral, of sorts, in Native worldviews. In keeping with Cheyenne tradition, the bride's wedding dress was made of buckskin by the bride's mother and maternal aunts. The groom, a non-Cheyenne, wore a business suit. The bride entered the ceremony riding a horse led by her father in a procession led by her mother. After a judge performed a civil marriage ceremony, a traditional Cheyenne ceremony that consisted of a simple blessing was offered by Richard Tall Bull, a Southern Cheyenne Wisdom Keeper or Elder.

The blessing was the center of the traditional Cheyenne ceremony. After completing the prayer, Mr. Tall Bull burned sacred cedar and fanned the smoke over the couple and then fanned it into the sky with a sacred eagle feather. This manner of offering prayers is widely shared by Native Peoples throughout North America. Cedar, sweet grass, sage and tobacco are often burned as sacraments when prayers are offered, and the eagle feather is an almost-universally shared sacred ceremonial item among Native Peoples. The power of the feather is closely associated with the power of the eagle, and the right to possess and use it is earned.

Another aspect of the traditional Cheyenne marriage ceremony is the strict traditions regarding relationships between the future wife and husband and their respective in-laws. In the Cheyenne tradition, the new husband should not interact with his new mother-in-law and her sisters (his wife's maternal aunts). By custom, they are to live as if they are "invisible" to each other. To a non-Native, this might appear rude. But in Cheyenne traditions, such conduct is deemed to be a way to ensure familial harmony.

Many Native Peoples have similar practices. Although it would be impolite for a guest to directly inquire about this behavior, careful observation will usually reveal whether the "invisibility" between certain persons is part of the customs of the Native Peoples you are visiting.

After the formal marriage ceremony, as in most religious faiths, a celebratory meal follows. Presents are welcomed by the newly married couple and are generally of a very practical nature, such as blankets, dishes, pots, pans and small household items. (In the case of Ms. Strange Owl-Raben's wedding, her mother gave the couple a traditional gift of a tipi, a dwelling that is central to living the Cheyenne way of life even today. Of course, the gift of a tipi would be fitting for plains tribes, but of little utility to any of the tribes of the Southwest or Southeast where tipis are not used.)

At a Native American/First Nations wedding ceremony, the bride and groom can be greeted with "Congratulations," plus a wish that they enjoy a happy and fruitful life together.

27

Orthodox Churches

(Includes the Antiochian Orthodox Church; the Carpatho-Russian Orthodox Church; the Greek Orthodox Church; the Orthodox Church in America [also known as the Russian Orthodox Church]; the Romanian Orthodox Church; the Serbian Orthodox Church; and the Ukrainian Orthodox Church. An entire chapter is devoted to Greek Orthodoxy in this book since it is the Orthodox denomination with the largest membership in the United States.)

HISTORY AND BELIEFS

The Orthodox Church, or the eastern half of the Christian Church, was formed in 1054 A.D. In that year the Great Schism occurred, causing a complete breakdown in communication and relations between the Roman Catholic Church, based in Rome, and the Orthodox Church, based in Constantinople. When the patriarchs of the various Orthodox churches meet, they are presided over by the Patriarch of Constantinople (present-day Istanbul), who is considered to be the "first among equals."

The term "Orthodox" is used to reflect adherents' belief that they believe and worship God correctly. Essentially, Orthodox Christians consider their beliefs similar to those of other Christian traditions, but believe that the balance and integrity of the teachings of Jesus' twelve apostles have been preserved inviolate by their Church.

Orthodoxy holds that the eternal truths of God's saving revelation in Jesus Christ are preserved in the living tradition of the Church under the guidance and inspiration of the Holy Spirit, which is the empowering spirit of God and the particular endowment of the Church. While the Holy

Scriptures are the written testimony of God's revelation, Holy Tradition is the all-encompassing experience of the Church under the guidance and direction of the Holy Spirit.

Orthodox churches are hierarchical and self-governing. They are also called "Eastern," because they stem from countries that shared the Christian heritage of the eastern part of the Roman and Byzantine Empire. They completely agree on matters of faith, despite a diversity of culture, language and the lands in which they flowered before arriving in North America.

Orthodox churches in North America today include:

- The American Carpatho-Russian Orthodox Greek Catholic Church, a self-governing diocese formalized in 1938 whose founders came from present-day Slovakia.
- The Antiochian Orthodox Christian Archdiocese of North America, an Arabic-language church whose first parish in North America was founded in Brooklyn in 1895. The Church in Antioch traces its origins to the days of the apostles, Peter and Paul, and to the Syrian city of Antioch in which the Book of Acts says the followers of Jesus Christ were first called "Christians."
- The Greek Orthodox Archdiocese of America, which is under the jurisdiction of the Ecumenical Patriarchate of Constantinople in Istanbul.
- The Orthodox Church in America, which was given full, independent status by the Russian Orthodox Church in 1970. It is comprised of ethnic Russians, Bulgarians, Albanians and Romanians.
- The Romanian Orthodox Church in America, which was founded in 1929 and was granted ecclesiastical autonomy in 1950 from the church in Romania.
- The Serbian Orthodox Church in the U.S.A. and Canada, which was created in 1921 and whose patriarchal seat is in Belgrade, Yugoslavia.
- The Ukrainian Orthodox Church of America, which was organized in 1928; and the Ukrainian Orthodox Church of Canada, which was organized in 1918, and which is the largest Ukrainian Orthodox Church beyond the borders of the Ukraine.

U.S. churches:

Antiochian Orthodox: 16
Carpatho-Russian Orthodox: 78
Greek Orthodox: 532
Romanian Orthodox: 37
Russian Orthodox (also known as the Orthodox Church
in America, or the OCA): 600

Serbian Orthodox: 68
Ukrainian Orthodox: 27

U.S. membership:

Antiochian Orthodox: 50,000
Carpatho-Russian Orthodox: 12,541
Greek Orthodox: 2 million
Romanian Orthodox: 65,000
Russian Orthodox (also known as the Orthodox Church
in America, or the OCA): 2 million
Serbian Orthodox: 67,000
Ukrainian Orthodox: 5,000

(*data from the respective denominations and from
the* 1998 Yearbook of American and Canadian Churches)

Canadian churches:

Antiochian Orthodox: 15
Greek Orthodox: 76
Romanian Orthodox: Not available
Russian Orthodox (also known as the Orthodox Church in
America): 606
Serbian Orthodox: Not available
Ukrainian Orthodox: 258

Canadian membership:

Antiochian Orthodox: 100,000
Greek Orthodox: 350,000
Romanian Orthodox: Not available
Russian Orthodox (also known as the Orthodox Church
in America): 1,000,000
Serbian Orthodox: Not available
Ukrainian Orthodox: 120,000

(*data from the* 1998 Yearbook of American and Canadian Churches)

MARRIAGE CEREMONY

To Orthodox Christians, marriage is a sacrament of union between man
and woman, who enter it to be mutually complemented and to propagate
the human race. In the Orthodox churches, rings are blessed and the bride
and groom each wear crowns during the ceremony to symbolize sacrifices
made in marriage, the priestly nature of marriage and the fact that the
bride and groom are now heads of their creation.

The 45- to 60-minute marriage ceremony is a ceremony in itself and not part of a larger service.

BEFORE THE CEREMONY

Are guests usually invited by a formal invitation?

Yes.

If not stated explicitly, should one assume that children are invited?

No.

If one can't attend, what should one do?

RSVP with regrets and send a gift.

APPROPRIATE ATTIRE

Men: A jacket and tie. No head covering is required.

Women: A dress or a skirt and blouse. Clothing should cover the arms and hems should reach below the knee. A head covering is not required. Open-toed shoes and modest jewelry may be worn.

There are no rules regarding colors of clothing.

GIFTS

Is a gift customarily expected?

Yes. Customarily, this may be cash or household goods.

Should gifts be brought to the ceremony?

Bring the gift to the ceremony or the reception or send it to the home of the newlyweds.

THE CEREMONY

Where will the ceremony take place?

In the main sanctuary of the church chosen by the celebrants and their family.

When should guests arrive and where should they sit?

It is customary to arrive either early or at the time for which the ceremony has been called. Ushers will advise guests on where to sit.

If arriving late, are there times when a guest should *not* enter the ceremony?

Do not enter during scripture readings and priestly blessings.

Are there times when a guest should *not* leave the ceremony?

No.

Who are the major officiants, leaders or participants at the ceremony and what do they do?

- *A bishop,* who is the chief celebrant.
- *A priest,* who may be the chief celebrant or the assistant to the bishop.
- *The deacon, sub-deacon and altar server,* all of whom assist the bishop or priest.
- *The bride and groom.*

What books are used?

In most Orthodox churches, only officiating bishops and priests use a text at a marriage ceremony.

To indicate the order of the ceremony:

A program will be distributed to congregants and guests.

Will a guest who is not a member of an Orthodox church be expected to do anything other than sit?

Stand when the congregants arise. Kneeling with them is appropriate only if it does not violate a visitor's own religious beliefs. Otherwise, visitors may sit when congregants kneel. Reading prayers aloud and singing with the congregants are optional.

Are there any parts of the ceremony in which a guest who is not a member of an Orthodox church should *not* participate?

No.

If not disruptive to the ceremony, is it okay to:

- **Take pictures?** Yes, but only with prior permission of a church official.
- **Use a flash?** Yes, but only with prior permission of a church official.
- **Use a video camera?** Yes, but only with prior permission of a church official.
- **Use a tape recorder?** Yes, but only with prior permission of a church official.

Will contributions to the church be collected at the ceremony?

No.

AFTER THE CEREMONY

Is there usually a reception after the ceremony?

Yes. This may last from one to four hours and may be held in the same building as the ceremony, at a catering hall or at the bride's parents' home. A meal will be served, often accompanied by alcoholic beverages.

Would it be considered impolite to neither eat nor drink?

No.

Is there a grace or benediction before eating or drinking?

Yes.

Is there a grace or benediction after eating or drinking?

No.

Is there a traditional greeting for the family?

In the Antiochian Orthodox Church, the traditional greeting for all occasions is "Mabbrook" ("MAB-brook"), which means "Blessings."
In the Romanian Orthodox Church, the traditional greeting is "La multi ani!" ("Lah MOOLTZ AH-nee"), which means "Many years!"
In other Orthodox churches, "Congratulations" is appropriate.

Is there a traditional form of address for clergy who may be at the reception?

"Father."

Is it okay to leave early?

Yes.

28

Pentecostal Church of God

HISTORY AND BELIEFS

The Pentecostal Church of God was founded in Chicago in 1919 by a group of participants in the then-current Pentecostal revival movement in the United States. Many people involved in the movement spontaneously spoke "in tongues" (or in a language unknown to those speaking it) and claims were made of divine healing that saved lives. Since many of these experiences were associated with the coming of the Holy Spirit (the empowering quality of God) on the Day of Pentecost, participants in the revival were called Pentecostals.

The group that met in Chicago was convinced that a formal Pentecostal church was necessary because many smaller, new, independent Pentecostal houses of worship had become the targets of small-time crooks and con men. They deemed their fledgling Pentecostal Church of God to be indispensable for the Pentecostal revival to continue to thrive.

Pentecostals tenaciously believe in their direct access to God, the Father, and believe prayer can manifest miracles. Worship services are demonstrative and energetic and are often marked by congregants speaking "in tongues." These are languages unknown to the speaker. Such speaking is interpreted as meaning that one is the recipient of the Holy Spirit. Alcohol and tobacco are prohibited to church members.

The Pentecostal Church of God has a combination of representative and congregational forms of government. While local churches are self-governing and elect their own ministers and local leaders, they are also expected to harmoniously function with the Church's district and general organization. The bylaws of local churches cannot conflict with the

148

Church's district or general bylaws. Each minister is accountable to his or her District Board in matters of faith and conduct.

The Church's biennial General Convention is its highest legislative body. Policy is made and governed by the Church's General Executive Board.

The Church's World Missions Department has ministers in 42 countries and maintains schools in most of these nations, as well. In addition, the Church's Indian Mission Department makes outreach to Native Americans.

Although the Pentecostal Church of God is not present within Canada, the broader Pentecostal tradition is well-represented by the Pentecostal Assemblies of Canada and the Pentecostal Assemblies of Newfoundland, which have a combined total of 1,257 churches, 234,000 members and offices in Mississauga, Ontario, and St. John's, Newfoundland, respectively.

U.S. churches: 1,230
U.S. membership: 111,900
(*data from the* 1998 Yearbook of American and Canadian Churches)

MARRIAGE CEREMONY

The Pentecostal Church of God teaches that the family was the first institution ordained by God in the Garden of Eden. The basis for a family is marriage between a man and a woman. Marriage, which is not to be entered into lightly, is said to be "until death do us part."

The marriage ceremony is a ceremony in itself and may last 30 to 60 minutes.

BEFORE THE CEREMONY

Are guests usually invited by a formal invitation?
Yes.

If not stated explicitly, should one assume that children are invited?
Yes.

If one can't attend, what should one do?
RSVP by card or letter with regrets and send a gift.

APPROPRIATE ATTIRE

Men: A jacket and tie or more casual attire, but not jeans or T-shirts. No head covering is required.

Women: A dress or a skirt and blouse. Clothing need not cover the arms and hems need not reach below the knees. Open-toed shoes and modest jewelry are permissible. No head covering is required.

There are no rules regarding colors of clothing.

GIFTS

Is a gift customarily expected?

Yes. Cash, savings bonds or small household items are most frequently given.

Should gifts be brought to the ceremony?

Gifts may either be brought to the ceremony or the reception afterward, or sent to the home of the newlyweds.

THE CEREMONY

Where will the ceremony take place?

In the sanctuary of the church.

When should guests arrive and where should they sit?

Arrive shortly before the time for which the ceremony has been called. Ushers will usually advise guests where to sit. Usually, the groom's family and friends sit on one side of the aisle and the bride's family and friends on the other.

If arriving late, are there times when a guest should *not* enter the ceremony?

Do not enter during the processional or recessional of the wedding party.

Are there times when a guest should *not* leave the ceremony?

Do not leave during the processional or recessional of the wedding party.

Who are the major officiants, leaders or participants at the ceremony and what do they do?

- *The minister,* who officiates.
- *The bride and groom and members of the wedding party.*

What books are used?

No books are used by the guests.

To indicate the order of the ceremony:

A program is sometimes distributed. If not, periodic announcements are made by the minister.

Will a guest who is not a member of the Pentecostal Church of God be expected to do anything other than sit?

Guests of other faiths are expected to stand when other guests arise during the ceremony.

Are there any parts of the ceremony in which a guest who is not a member of the Pentecostal Church of God should *not* participate?

No.

If not disruptive to the ceremony, is it okay to:

◪ **Take pictures?** Yes, but only with prior permission of the minister.
◪ **Use a flash?** Yes, but only with prior permission of the minister.
◪ **Use a video camera?** Yes, but only with prior permission of the minister.
◪ **Use a tape recorder?** Yes.

Will contributions to the church be collected at the ceremony?

No.

AFTER THE CEREMONY

Is there usually a reception after the ceremony?

Yes. It may be in the same building where the wedding ceremony was held or in a catering hall. Receptions usually include light food, such as finger foods, cake, mints, nuts and punch. There will be no alcoholic beverages or dancing, although there might be music. The reception may last 30 to 60 minutes.

Would it be considered impolite to neither eat nor drink?

No.

Is there a grace or benediction before eating or drinking?

No.

Is there a grace or benediction after eating or drinking?

No.

Is there a traditional greeting for the family?

Just offer your congratulations.

Is there a traditional form of address for clergy who may be at the reception?

"Pastor," "Minister" or "Brother."

Is it okay to leave early?

Yes.

29

Presbyterian

HISTORY AND BELIEFS

The Presbyterian Church was founded on the ideals of the Protestant Reformation and based on the concept of democratic rule under the authority of God. John Calvin (1509-1564) is the father of Presbyterianism.

All Presbyterians are required to trust in Christ as their forgiving savior, promise to follow Christ and His example for living, and commit themselves to attend church and to become involved in its work. They believe in the Holy Spirit (the empowering presence of God) speaking through the Bible, and in the sanctity of life.

Presbyterian theology emphasizes the majesty of God, who is conceived not just as truth or beauty, but also as intention, purpose, energy and will. The human counterpart of this is understanding the Christian life as the embodiment of the purposes of God and the working out of these purposes in one's life. Because of this, Presbyterians include many social activists, and those who try to shape and influence culture and history.

The Presbyterian Church (USA) was formed when the Presbyterian Church in the United States merged in 1983 with the United Presbyterian Church in the United States of America. The consolidation ended a schism that occurred during the Civil War when Southern Presbyterians broke away from the Presbyterian Church in the United States of America to create the Presbyterian Church in the Confederate States. Today's Presbyterian Church is the result of at least 10 different denominational mergers over the last 250 years and is strongly ecumenical in outlook.

The Presbyterian Church in Canada was formed in 1875 by the union of four branches of Presbyterianism that had been established as

Europeans settled the country. The church experienced remarkable growth during the next 50 years, reaching almost 1.5 million members, the largest church in the country of 8.7 million people. Presbyterians had initiated discussions with the Methodist and Congregationalist churches, leading to the formation of the United Church of Canada in 1925. But a third of Presbyterians were not satisfied with the final plans and stayed out of the new denomination.

U. S. churches: 11,328
U. S. membership: 3.6 million
(*data from the* 1998 Yearbook of American and Canadian Churches)

Canadian churches: 1,010
Canadian membership: 145,328
(*data from the* 1998 Yearbook of American and Canadian Churches)

MARRIAGE CEREMONY

Presbyterians consider the marital relationship as sacred, but the wedding ceremony is not a sacrament. For Presbyterians, there are only two sacraments: Baptism and communion.

The wedding ceremony varies widely, but generally follows the order of worship used by the church during Sunday services, with the addition of exchanging rings and vows. The wedding ceremony takes 30 to 60 minutes.

BEFORE THE CEREMONY

Are guests usually invited by a formal invitation?
Yes.

If not stated explicitly, should one assume that children are invited?
No.

If one can't attend, what should one do?
RSVP with regrets and send a gift or card.

APPROPRIATE ATTIRE

Men: Jacket and tie or, at the discretion of the individual, more casual clothing. No head covering is required.

Women: Dress or a skirt and blouse or, at the discretion of the individual, more casual clothing. Open-toed shoes and modest jewelry permitted.

Hems need not reach the knees nor must arms be covered. No head covering is required.

There are no rules regarding colors of clothing.

GIFTS

Is a gift customarily expected?

Yes, usually such gifts as household items (towels, sheets, small appliances) are appropriate.

Should gifts be brought to the ceremony?

Gifts should be sent to the home of the newlyweds or brought to the reception.

THE CEREMONY

Where will the ceremony take place?

In the church.

When should guests arrive and where should they sit?

Arrive on time. An usher will show guests where to sit.

If arriving late, are there times when a guest should *not* enter the ceremony?

Follow the usher's cues for entering the service. Do not enter during the procession or recession of the wedding party.

Are there times when a guest should *not* leave the ceremony?

Do not leave during the procession or recession of the wedding party.

Who are the major officiants, leaders or participants at the ceremony and what do they do?

◼ *The pastor or minister,* who leads the service.
◼ *The bride and groom and the members of the wedding party.*

What books are used?

In the U.S., the two main books in the service are a hymnal and a Bible. Since there are no prescribed editions of either, hymnals and the version of the Bible may differ from one congregation to another. The most recent edition of the Old and New Testaments recommended for Presbyterians is the New Revised Standard Version, which is printed by several publishers. The most recent hymnal is the *Presbyterian Hymnal* (Louisville, Ky.: Westminster/John Knox Press, 1990). No individual Presbyterian or individual Presbyterian church is required to use these.

In Canada, the two main books in worship are *The Book of Praise* and the Bible. *The Book of Praise* contains the hymns sung by the congregation. There is also growing use of a Psalter (1997) that allows for the Psalms to be read or (in very few churches) chanted.

To indicate the order of the ceremony:
The pastor or minister will make announcements as the service proceeds. A printed program or bulletin for the service may be distributed.

Will a guest who is not a Presbyterian be expected to do anything other than sit?
Nothing is "expected" of guests. If they wish, they may stand, sing and pray with the congregation, if this does not compromise their own religious beliefs.

Are there any parts of the ceremony in which a guest who is not a Presbyterian should *not* participate?
No.

If not disruptive to the ceremony, is it okay to:
- **Take pictures?** Yes.
- **Use a flash?** No.
- **Use a video camera?** Yes.
- **Use a tape recorder?** Yes.

Will contributions to the church be collected at the ceremony?
No.

AFTER THE CEREMONY

Is there usually a reception after the ceremony?
There is usually a one- to two-hour reception, with eating, drinking and toasting. Alcoholic beverages will probably be served. There may also be dancing and music.

It may be in a church hall, a catering facility or another place chosen by the bride and groom.

Would it be considered impolite to neither eat nor drink?
No.

Is there a grace or benediction before eating or drinking?
Depends on local preferences.

Is there a grace or benediction after eating or drinking?
No.

Is there a traditional greeting for the family?

Just offer your congratulations to the bride and groom and their immediate family.

Is there a traditional form of address for clergy who may be at the reception?

"Reverend," followed by the pastor's last name. In Canada, simply "Mr." or "Ms." followed by the minister's last name; not "Reverend."

Is it okay to leave early?

Depends on local preferences.

30

Quaker
(Religious Society of Friends)

HISTORY AND BELIEFS

The name *Quaker* was originally a nickname for the Children of Light or the Friends of Truth, as they called themselves. Members of the group were said to tremble or quake with religious zeal, and the nickname stuck. In time, they came to be known simply as "Friends."

The central Quaker conviction is that the saving knowledge and power of God are present as divine influences in each person through what has been variously called the "inner light," the "light of the eternal Christ within" or "the Seed within." Many affirm their acceptance of Jesus as their personal savior. Others conceive of the inward guide as a universal spirit that was in Jesus in abundant nature and is in everyone to some degree.

This reliance on the Spirit within was a direct challenge to religions that relied on outward authority, such as Catholicism or mainstream Protestantism. Largely because of this, Quakers were persecuted from the time they were founded in England in the 1650s. This tapered off about four decades later, and the English Quakers continued to grow and establish Quaker meetings, or congregations, in many parts of the world, especially in the British colonies in North America.

Quakers do not have ordained ministers and do not celebrate outward Christian sacraments. They seek, instead, an inward reality and contend that all life is sacramental.

Belief in the "inner light" present in every person also accounts for the distinctive nature of unprogrammed Quaker worship, in which the congregation is silent except when individuals are moved to speak. This conviction also motivates Quaker confidence in working for the kingdom of God in this world and their emphasis over the years on nonviolence and peace, abolishing slavery, relieving suffering, improving housing, educational and employment opportunities, reforming prisons and eliminating prejudice and discrimination against minorities and the underprivileged.

Quakers are strongly opposed to war and conscription and seek to remove the causes of war and conflict. While a few Quakers have accepted the draft and fought in wars, most declare themselves to be conscientious objectors. A small minority are draft resisters, and refuse to register or in any way cooperate with the military system.

U.S. meetings or congregations: 1,200
U.S. membership: 104,000
(*data from the* 1998 Yearbook of American and Canadian Churches)

Canadian meetings or worship groups: 57
Canadian membership: 1,126
(*data from Reports, Ottawa: Canadian Yearly Meeting, 1998*)

MARRIAGE CEREMONY

From its beginnings, the Religious Society of Friends has stressed the belief that marriage is a binding relationship entered into in the presence of God and of witnessing friends. Before this public commitment is made on the day of the wedding, the proposed marriage has already received the approval of the Monthly Meeting, which is given after careful consideration by an appointed committee.

A Quaker marriage ceremony has the form of a regular "meeting," or worship service, but during it the bride and groom exchange vows and sign a marriage certificate. The certificate, which is a religious document, is read aloud, and then the meeting continues. There is also a legal marriage certificate which is witnessed by two members of the meeting's oversight committee.

There are two types of Quaker meetings: "Unprogrammed" and "programmed." Unprogrammed meetings are held in the traditional manner of the Friends on the basis of silence. Worshippers sit and wait for divine guidance and inspiration. If so moved, they then speak to the group. This is called "vocal ministry."

Programmed meetings are planned in advance and usually include hymn singing, vocal prayers, Bible reading, silent worship and a sermon.

In many cases, worship is led by a pastor, who is generally paid and is responsible for some other pastoral services in the meeting.

The marriage ceremony may last 30 to 60 minutes.

BEFORE THE CEREMONY

Are guests usually invited by a formal invitation?
Yes.

If not stated explicitly, should one assume that children are invited?
Yes.

If one can't attend, what should one do?
RSVP with your regrets. Possibly send a gift.

APPROPRIATE ATTIRE

Men: Jacket and tie or more informal clothing. Varies with each ceremony. No head covering is required.

Women: A dress or a skirt and blouse or a pants suit. Open-toed shoes and modest jewelry are permissible. Varies with each ceremony. No head covering is required.

There are no rules regarding colors of clothing.

GIFTS

Is a gift customarily expected?
Yes—anything the giver deems appropriate or which is requested by the newlyweds. Some couples may suggest that contributions be given to a certain charity or cause; others may register with a bridal registry.

Should gifts be brought to the ceremony?
Usually they are sent to the home of the newlyweds.

THE CEREMONY

Where will the ceremony take place?
Depending on the wishes of the bride and groom, it may be in their meetinghouse or in a home or outdoors.

When should guests arrive and where should they sit?
Arrive early. Ushers will probably advise guests on where to sit. The front rows tend to be reserved for immediate members of the two families.

If arriving late, are there times when a guest should *not* enter the ceremony?
If someone is offering a vocal ministry, wait until he or she has finished.

Are there times when a guest should *not* leave the ceremony?
It is inappropriate to leave, especially during vocal ministry.

Who are the major officiants, leaders or participants and what do they do?
Members of the meeting or friends or relatives of the bride and groom will:
- Bring the wedding certificate to the couple, who are usually at the front of the room.
- Be appointed by the oversight committee in consultation with the couple to read the wedding certificate aloud to the guests.
- Be asked by the oversight committee in consultation with the couple to briefly explain the procedure of the ceremony to those assembled.
- Close the meeting. This is usually done by those at the front of the room who had explained the purpose of marriage shaking each other's hands. This is followed by guests shaking hands with those near them.

What books are used?
A Bible or a hymnal.

To indicate the order of the ceremony:
A verbal explanation of the service is usually sufficient.

Will a guest who is not a Quaker be expected to do anything other than sit?
No, but guests are welcome to speak if moved to do so. All present should sign the marriage certificate afterward. This is usually placed in the meeting room and can be signed after the close of worship.

Are there any parts of the ceremony in which a guest who is not a Quaker should *not* participate?
No.

If not disruptive to the ceremony, is it okay to:
- **Take pictures?** No.
- **Use a flash?** No.
- **Use a video camera?** No.
- **Use a tape recorder?** Possibly. Ask permission from the couple.
(Photos and videos are usually taken after the ceremony.)

Will contributions to the meeting be collected at the ceremony?
No.

AFTER THE CEREMONY

Is there usually a reception after the ceremony?

There is often a reception that may last one to two hours. It may be at a home, at a catering facility or at any other site chosen by the family. The extent of the food that is served varies from wedding to wedding. Some may have light food and beverages. Others may have a sit-down meal. Still others may have a pot-luck meal. Often, no alcohol is served, mostly because there was a Quaker tradition during most of the 19th century and the first half of the 20th century advising Friends to abstain from drinking alcohol.

Depending on the newlyweds' preferences, there may be music and/or dancing.

Would it be considered impolite to neither eat nor drink?

No.

Is there a grace or benediction before eating or drinking?

There may be a silent or spoken grace if the reception is a "sit-down" affair.

Is there a grace or benediction after eating or drinking?

No.

Is there a traditional greeting for the family?

Offer your congratulations.

Is there a traditional form of address for clergy who may be at the reception?

No.

Is it okay to leave early?

Yes, but usually only after the wedding cake is cut and served.

31

Reformed Church in America/Canada

HISTORY AND BELIEFS

The Reformed Church began in the 1500s in Europe when groups of Christians who were opposed to any authority or practice that they believed could not be supported by a careful study of the Bible set themselves apart from the established Roman Church of the time. These Reformers adhered to the basic teachings of the early Christian church, but they also wrote new teachings, such as the Heidelberg Catechism, which was first published in 1563 and is still a standard that guides the life and religious witness of the Reformed Church in America.

The tone of the Heidelberg Catechism is mild, gentle and devotional, and celebrates the comfort that one can derive in life and in death from Jesus Christ. The Reformed Church in America requires every minister to cover the contents of the Heidelberg Catechism once every four years in his or her preaching.

The Reform movement's first church in America was the Reformed Dutch Church, which was founded in 1628 in New Amsterdam (now New York City). Not until 1764 was there a Reformed Church in the British colonies that used the English language. Starting with the American Revolution, the Dutch influence in the Church waned as the number of congregants of Scottish, German and English extraction increased. Finally, in 1867, the Church changed its name to the Reformed Church in America.

The Canadian branch of the denomination, which consists of 41 churches, is called the Reformed Church in Canada. (The Reform tradition is also represented in Canada by the Christian Reformed Church of North

America, which has 244 churches, a membership of 47,000 and offices in Burlington, Ontario.)

Each of the Reformed Church's local congregations is governed by a "consistory," which is comprised of the church's pastor and elected elders and deacons. Each church belongs to a "classis," which oversees the congregations within its particular jurisdiction. Each classis sends representatives to its regional synod, of which there are seven in the United States and one in Canada. It also sends representatives to the General Synod, which meets annually to set direction and policy for the Church as a whole.

The Church now supports missionaries on five continents. While the Church has been making concerted outreach to non-whites in the United States in recent years, its membership is still predominantly people with an Anglo-Saxon heritage: 95 percent of Church members are Caucasian; four percent are African-American; and two percent are Asian, Native American or Hispanic.

U.S. and Canadian churches: 950
U.S. and Canadian membership: 310,603
(*data from the* 1998 Yearbook of American and Canadian Churches)

MARRIAGE CEREMONY

The Reformed Church teaches that the essence of marriage is a covenanted commitment that has its foundation in the faithfulness of God's love. The Church does not consider a wedding to be a sacrament, although the marital relationship is considered to be sacred.

The marriage ceremony is the occasion on which two people unite as husband and wife in the mutual exchange of marriage vows and wedding rings. The presiding official represents the Church and gives the marriage the Church's blessing. The congregation joins in affirming the marriage and in offering support and thanksgiving for the new family.

Usually, the wedding is a ceremony in itself. Only rarely is it part of a regular Sunday worship service. It may last about 30 minutes.

BEFORE THE CEREMONY

Are guests usually invited by a formal invitation?

Yes.

If not stated explicitly, should one assume that children are invited?

Yes, although this may not apply to infants or toddlers.

If one can't attend, what should one do?

RSVP with regrets and send a gift.

APPROPRIATE ATTIRE

Men: A jacket and tie. No head covering is required.

Women: A dress or a skirt and blouse. Clothing need not cover the arms and hems need not reach below the knees. Open-toed shoes and modest jewelry are permissible. No head covering is required.

There are no rules regarding colors of clothing.

GIFTS

Is a gift customarily expected?

Yes. Cash or household items (such as sheets, kitchenware or small appliances) are appropriate.

Should gifts be brought to the ceremony?

Gifts may be brought to the ceremony or to the reception that follows the ceremony. They may also be sent to the home of the newlyweds.

THE CEREMONY

Where will the ceremony take place?

In the church's main sanctuary.

When should guests arrive and where should they sit?

Arrive shortly before the time for which the wedding has been scheduled. Usually, ushers will advise guests where to sit.

If arriving late, are there times when a guest should *not* enter the ceremony?

Do not enter during the processional or recessional of the wedding party or during the recitation of wedding vows. Follow the ushers' guidance for entering the ceremony.

Are there times when a guest should *not* leave the ceremony?

Do not leave during the processional or recessional of the wedding party or during the recitation of wedding vows. Follow the ushers' guidance for leaving the ceremony.

Who are the major officiants, leaders or participants at the ceremony and what do they do?

- *The pastor,* who presides over the ceremony.
- *The bride and groom and members of the wedding party.*

What books are used?

The most commonly used of several Protestant Bibles is the New Revised Standard Version. The Reformed Church in America does not recommend a particular edition of this Bible. Many hymnals are used in the Reformed Church. The most recent hymnal published by the Church is *Rejoice in the Lord,* edited by Erik Routley (Grand Rapids, Mich.: William B. Eerdmans Publishing Co., 1985).

To indicate the order of the ceremony:

The pastor will make periodic announcements.

Will a guest who is not a member of the Reformed Church be expected to do anything other than sit?

Guests are expected to join congregants when they stand during the ceremony.

Are there any parts of the ceremony in which a guest who is not a member of the Reformed Church should *not* participate?

No.

If not disruptive to the ceremony, is it okay to:

- **Take pictures?** No.
- **Use a flash?** No.
- **Use a video camera?** No.
- **Use a tape recorder?** No.

Will contributions to the church be collected at the ceremony?

No.

AFTER THE CEREMONY

Is there usually a reception after the ceremony?

Yes. It may be in a catering hall, a restaurant or a church reception hall, or at a home. There is usually a reception line and frequently a full meal is served. If the reception is not in the church, there may be alcoholic beverages and/or music and dancing. The presence of alcoholic beverages depends on family practice and choice. The reception may last one to two hours.

Would it be considered impolite to neither eat nor drink?

No.

Is there a grace or benediction before eating or drinking?

Grace may be said if a full meal is served.

Is there a grace or benediction after eating or drinking?

No.

Is there a traditional greeting for the family?

Just offer your congratulations.

Is there a traditional form of address for clergy who may be at the reception?

"Pastor" or "Reverend."

Is it okay to leave early?

Yes.

32

Roman Catholic

HISTORY AND BELIEFS

The term "catholic" was first applied around 100 A.D. to the Christian Church, which was then one entity. It meant being geographically universal, continuous with the Christian past and transcending language, race and nation. The test of catholicity was communion with the universal Church and with the See of Rome.

After the eastern and western wings of the church divided in 1054 A.D., "catholic" was more usually used to refer to the church in the west under the spiritual leadership of the Holy See based in Rome. (This is commonly known as the Vatican.) Since the 16th century, "Roman Catholic" has meant the religious body which acknowledges the pope's authority and the Vatican as the center of ecclesiastical unity.

In the 19th century, the church became increasingly centralized in Rome. In 1870, Vatican Council I declared that the pope has jurisdictional primacy over the entire church, and that under certain circumstances, he is infallible in proclaiming doctrines of faith and morals.

In Roman Catholic teaching, revelation is summed up in Jesus Christ, who commanded his apostles to teach the gospel. To preserve the living gospel, the apostles appointed bishops as their successors. Roman Catholics believe in the unity of God, who is understood as God the Father, God the Son (Jesus Christ) and God the Holy Spirit. Catholicism teaches that original sin—Adam and Eve's expulsion from the Garden of Eden for disobeying God—alienated humanity from God, but did not totally corrupt man and woman, and that grace can fully make a sinner just.

Catholics especially venerate Mary, the mother of Jesus. Catholics believe that Mary was conceived without original sin, and that she was a virgin when Jesus was conceived.

Roman Catholicism has about 900 million members in 2,000 dioceses around the world.

U.S. churches: 22,728
U.S. membership: 61.2 million
(*data from the* 1998 Yearbook of American and Canadian Churches)

Canadian churches: 5,706
Canadian membership: 12.5 million
(*data from the* 1998 Yearbook of American and Canadian Churches)

MARRIAGE CEREMONY

Catholics consider married life, which was created by God, to have a decisive bearing on the continuation of the human race, on the personal development and eternal destiny of individual members of a family, and on the dignity, stability, peace and prosperity of families and society.

Love, the church teaches, is uniquely expressed and perfected through marriage. Children are the "gift of marriage," although marriage is not instituted solely for procreation. Rather, its essential nature as an unbreakable compact between man and wife and for the welfare of the children that come out of it both demand that the love of the respective spouses be embodied in a manner that grows, thrives and ripens.

The marriage ceremony may either be a ceremony in itself and not part of a larger service or it may be part of a mass. It may last between 30 and 60 minutes to more than one hour.

BEFORE THE CEREMONY

Are guests usually invited by a formal invitation?
Yes.

If not stated explicitly, should one assume that children are invited?
Yes.

If one can't attend, what should one do?
RSVP with regrets and send a gift.

APPROPRIATE ATTIRE

Men: Jacket and tie or more relaxed clothing. No head covering required.

Women: Dress or a skirt and blouse or a pants suit. Jewelry and open-toed shoes are acceptable. Clothing should be modest, depending on the fashion and the locale. No head covering required. It is recommended that black not be worn.

GIFTS

Is a gift customarily expected?
Yes. Often money is most appropriate, with the exact amount subject to your discretion.

Should gifts be brought to the ceremony?
Gifts should be sent to the home or brought to the reception.

THE CEREMONY

Where will the ceremony take place?
In the main sanctuary of the church.

When should guests arrive and where should they sit?
Arrive on time. An usher will show guests where to sit.

Are there times when a guest should *not* enter the ceremony?
Ushers may guide latecomers. Do not enter as the wedding party processes into the sanctuary.

Are there times when a guest should *not* leave the service?
Do not leave until it ends.

Who are the major officiants, leaders or participants at the ceremony and what do they do?
◗ *The priest,* who witnesses the vows.
◗ *The bride and groom and their wedding party.*

What books are used?
The hymnal, the New American Bible (or another authorized translation) or a lectionary that contains selections from the Bible, and a prayer book, which is also called a missal.

To indicate the order of the ceremony:
There will be a program.

Will a guest who is not a Catholic be expected to do anything other than sit?
Guests are expected to stand with the congregation. It is optional for them to kneel, read prayers aloud or sing with the congregation.

Are there any parts of the ceremony in which a non-Catholic guest should *not* participate?
Non-Catholics do not receive communion.

If not disruptive to the ceremony, is it okay to:
◘ **Take pictures?** Yes. Verify beforehand with the priest or usher.
◘ **Use a flash?** Yes. Verify beforehand with the priest or usher.
◘ **Use a video camera?** Yes. Verify beforehand with the priest or usher.
◘ **Use a tape recorder?** Yes. Verify beforehand with the priest or usher.

Will contributions to the church be collected at the ceremony?
No.

AFTER THE CEREMONY

Is there usually a reception after the ceremony?
There is a reception that may last more than two hours. It is usually at a catering hall, where food and beverages will be served and there will be dancing and music.

Would it be considered impolite to neither eat nor drink?
No.

Is there a grace or benediction before eating or drinking?
Yes, the blessing before the meal.

Is there a grace or benediction after eating or drinking?
Usually not.

Is there a traditional greeting for the family?
Just offer your congratulations.

Is there a traditional form of address for clergy who may be at the reception?
"Father" if greeting a priest. "Your excellency" if greeting a bishop. "Your eminence" if greeting a cardinal.

Is it okay to leave early?
Yes.

33

Seventh-day Adventist

HISTORY AND BELIEFS

The Seventh-day Adventist Church stemmed from a worldwide religious revival in the mid-1800s when people of many faiths fervently believed biblical prophecies that they interpreted as meaning that Jesus Christ's second coming, or "advent," was imminent.

When Christ did not come in the 1840s, a group of these disappointed Adventists in the U.S. concluded that they had misinterpreted prophetic events, and that the second coming was still in the future. This same group later became known as Seventh-day Adventists, which organized formally as a denomination in 1863.

Adventists anticipate and prepare for the world's end in conjunction with the second coming of Jesus Christ. They believe that the end of the world is near and that eternal hell for the wicked is not consistent with the concept of a "loving Father." Instead, they believe in eventual annihilation of the wicked and eternal bliss for the saved. After a thousand-year reign of the saints with Christ in Heaven, the wicked will be raised and, along with Satan, annihilated. Out of the chaos of the old earth will emerge a new earth, which the redeemed will inherit as their everlasting home.

Worldwide, there are about eight million Seventh-day Adventists. The movement grows by about seven percent annually and has more than 37,000 congregations in over 200 countries.

In addition to a mission program, the church has the largest worldwide Protestant parochial school system with over 800,000 elementary through college students in more than 5,400 schools. It also operates medical schools and hospitals.

U.S. churches: 4,363
U.S. membership: 809,000

(*data from the* 1998 Yearbook of American and Canadian Churches)

Canadian churches: 336
Canadian membership: 46,961

(*data from 1997*)

MARRIAGE CEREMONY

Seventh-day Adventists believe that marriage was divinely established in Eden. To accomplish this most important part of Creation, God performed a miracle and brought forth Eve from the side of Adam, and gave her to Adam as his wife. Jesus later affirmed marriage to be a lifelong union between a man and a woman in loving companionship.

A marriage commitment is to God, as well as to the spouse. Marriage should be entered into only between partners who share a common religious faith. Mutual love, honor, respect and responsibility are the fabric of this relationship.

The marriage ceremony usually lasts between 30 and 60 minutes.

BEFORE THE CEREMONY

Are guests usually invited by a formal invitation?
Yes. Occasionally, there will be a general invitation in the local church bulletin.

If not stated explicitly, should one assume that children are invited?
Yes.

If one can't attend, what should one do?
RSVP with your regrets and send a gift to the bride and groom.

APPROPRIATE ATTIRE

Men: Jacket and tie. No head covering required.

Women: Dress or skirt and blouse. No head covering required. Clothing should cover the arms and hems should reach below the knee.

Although Adventists do not ordinarily wear jewelry, guests should feel comfortable wearing it.

There are no rules regarding colors of clothing.

GIFTS

Is a gift customarily expected?
Only if the celebrants are close friends or relatives. Money and other gifts are appropriate.

Should gifts be brought to the ceremony?
Gifts may be sent to the home before or after the wedding ceremony or brought to the ceremony and placed in the reception area.

THE CEREMONY

Where will the ceremony take place?
In a variety of settings, although most commonly in the church sanctuary.

When should guests arrive and where should they sit?
Arrive shortly before the ceremony is scheduled to start.

If arriving late, are there times when a guest should *not* enter the ceremony?
Latecomers should not enter during the bride's entry.

Are there times when a guest should *not* leave the ceremony?
Do not leave during prayer.

Who are the major officiants, leaders or participants at the ceremony and what do they do?
- *The pastor,* who will deliver a few comments.
- *The bride and groom and their wedding party.*

What books are used?
Only the clergyman uses a Bible.

To indicate the order of the ceremony:
A program will be distributed.

Will a guest who is not a Seventh-day Adventist be expected to do anything other than sit?
It is optional for guests to stand, kneel and sing with the congregation.

Are there any parts of the ceremony in which a guest who is not a Seventh-day Adventist should *not* participate?
Guests who belong to other faiths can participate in all aspects of the service, unless restricted from doing so by their own faith.

If not disruptive to the ceremony, is it okay to:
- **Take photographs?** Yes.
- **Use a flash?** Yes.
- **Use a video camera?** Yes.
- **Use a tape recorder?** Yes.

Will contributions to the church be collected at the ceremony?
No.

AFTER THE CEREMONY

Is there usually a reception after the ceremony?
There is usually a 30- to 60-minute reception. The location varies, but will be announced in advance. Guests greet the participants, visit with other guests and enjoy the food. Usually, there is punch and cake. Sometimes, there is a sit-down meal. There will be no alcoholic beverages.

Would it be considered impolite to neither eat nor drink?
No, especially if a guest has dietary restrictions.

Is there a grace or benediction before eating or drinking?
Wait for a brief prayer of thanks for the food before eating.

Is there a grace or benediction after eating or drinking?
No.

Is there a special greeting for the family?
Just offer your congratulations.

Is there a traditional form of address for clergy who may be at the reception?
"Elder" or "Pastor."

Is it okay to leave early?
Yes.

34
Sikh

The Sikh faith originated in India in the late 15th century through the life and teachings of Guru Nanak (1469–1539), the first Sikh guru. At a time of great religious conflict, he taught that all creation is a part of the One Creator. After Guru Nanak's life, he passed his "light" on successively to nine other gurus who further evolved his teachings. Each guru denounced India's caste system and the oppression of anyone based on class, creed, color or sex.

The 10th and last human guru, Guru Gobind Singh, initiated his followers as the *Khalsa*, which means "the Pure Ones." He instructed the *Khalsa* not to cut their hair (since doing so would tamper with God's image, in which they were created); to dress in white Sikh attire called *bana*, which consists of turbans and dress-like garments called *kurtas* and leggings called *churidars*; to be monogamous; and to live righteously. Before dying in 1708, Guru Gobind Singh "gave" the guruship to the Sikh scriptures known as the *Siri Guru Granth Sahib*. These scriptures were compiled by the fifth guru, Arjan Dev, and contain sacred writings by some Sikh gurus and several Hindu and Moslem saints. Since then, Sikhs have bowed before the *Siri Guru Granth Sahib*, consulted it as their only guru and treated it with reverence.

Today, there are 20 million Sikhs throughout the world.

U.S. temples/*gurdwaras*: 260
U.S. membership: 305,000
(1996 data from Sikh Dharma International)

175

**Canadian temples/*gurdwaras:* 100
Canadian membership:** 300,000
(data from Sikh Society of Alberta, Edmonton, Alberta)

MARRIAGE CEREMONY

A couple is considered to come together in a Sikh marriage to help each other on the spiritual path. The merging of two identities that takes place in a marriage is an earthly symbol for the more infinite merger between the soul and God.

A wedding can take place as part of the regular *gurdwara* service, but it may be a service unto itself. One or more couples may be married at the same time. A minister addresses the *sangat* (the congregation), then explains to the couple the Sikh concept of marriage and commitment. The bride and groom will be called to sit in front of the *Siri Guru Granth Sahib*, the Sikh holy book. The *kirtanis* (musicians) will be seated on one side and the minister on the other side at the front of the *gurdwara*, the Sikh place of worship.

A short prayer called an *ardas* is recited to bless the wedding. Only immediate family and the wedding couple stand at this time. A *hukam*, or "Guru's command," for the wedding is then read from the *Siri Guru Granth Sahib*. Next, a special shawl is placed on the shoulder of the groom and in the hands of the bride. The shawl links the couple throughout the wedding ceremony.

The couple is considered to be married when they have circled the *Siri Guru Granth Sahib* four times after reciting four "marriage rounds," which are special verses from the *Siri Guru Granth Sahib*, in Gurmukhi and then in English (or the primary language of the *sangat*, the congregation). The rounds are then sung by the *kirtanis*. These marriage rounds were written by the fourth Sikh guru for his own wedding in the 16th century. They include special instructions for married life. During these rounds, family and close friends (including non-Sikh guests) may be invited to stand around the *Siri Guru Granth Sahib* to show their support for the couple whom they also encircle. In some *gurdwaras*, as the couple finishes the last round, the congregation may shower the couple with flower petals to show joy and congratulations. At this point, the couple is officially considered to be married and the minister may then make a legal pronouncement of marriage.

The first act of the newly married couple is to feed each other fruit. This illustrates their commitment to nourish and support each other.

If the wedding ceremony is part of a full worship service, the couple and their family and friends now rejoin the *sangat* and the service proceeds as usual.

The wedding itself usually lasts about one hour.

BEFORE THE CEREMONY

Are guests usually invited by a formal invitation?

Possibly, but not always. Sikh weddings are open to everyone.

If not stated explicitly, should one assume that children are invited?

Yes.

If one can't attend, what should one do?

Respond in writing or call, and send a gift if you desire to do so.

APPROPRIATE ATTIRE

Men: A jacket and tie or more casual, modest clothing. Shoes are always removed before entering the *gurdwara*, and the head must always be covered while in the *gurdwara*. Guests may wear any hat, cap, or scarf that covers the top of the head.

Women: A modest dress, skirt and blouse, or pants suit. It is best if the legs are covered enough so one can comfortably sit cross-legged. Shoes are always removed before entering the *gurdwara*, and the head must always be covered with a scarf, hat or veil which covers the top of the head while in the *gurdwara*. Modest jewelry is permissible.

There are no rules regarding colors of clothing.

GIFTS

Is a gift customarily expected?

There is no Sikh tradition dictating gift giving for weddings. If one wishes to present a gift, appropriate gifts may include household items (such as sheets, kitchenware or small appliances), a special, inspirational gift or money.

Should gifts be brought to the ceremony?

Gifts may either be left in the entry room or brought to a later reception.

THE CEREMONY

Where will the ceremony take place?

In the main *gurdwara*.

When should guests arrive and where should they sit?

Arrive shortly before the time for which the ceremony has been called, although some *gurdwaras* with primarily Eastern Indian congregants begin weddings much later than what is indicated on an invitation, so it's best to inquire of your host beforehand when the ceremony will actually start.

As with all *gurdwara* services, everyone sits facing the *Siri Guru Granth Sahib*, sometimes with the men on the left and women on the right.

If arriving late, are there times when a guest should *not* enter the ceremony?

A guest may enter at any time during the service, except during the *ardas* (community prayer), which is the point during the service when everyone is standing. One should wait at the entrance to the main worship room until these prayers have ended.

Are there times when a guest should *not* leave the ceremony?

It is advised not to leave during the *ardas* (prayer), *hukam* (the reading from the *Siri Guru Granth Sahib*) or the "wedding rounds," which are special verses from the *Siri Guru Granth Sahib* recited by the couple in Gurmukhi and then in English (or the primary language of the *sangat*, the congregation).

Guests may wish to sit near the door if they plan on leaving the ceremony early.

Who are the major officiants, leaders or participants at the ceremony and what do they do?

- *The Granthi or Giani Ji*, the person reading the *hukam*, or portion, from the *Siri Guru Granth Sahib*. He or she also reads the four wedding rounds.
- *The minister*, the person who officiates at the wedding ceremony.
- *The bride and groom and their wedding party.*
- *Kirtanis*, musicians who lead the *sangat*, or congregation, in *kirtan* (songs of praise to God).

What books are used?

Booklets of sheets (containing transliteration and translation of the *kirtan* to be sung) may be available, depending on the *gurdwara*. These are often found at the front of the *gurdwara* and in front of the *Siri Guru Granth Sahib*. Effort should be made not to place these booklets on the floor. Since

Sikhs respect the written word of God, anything containing it should not be stepped upon or marred in any way.

To indicate the order of the ceremony:

There may be a written program and/or the master of ceremonies may make periodic announcements.

Will a guest who is not a Sikh be expected to do anything other than sit?

A guest is expected to stand and sit at the same time as everyone else, but it is optional to sing or bow to the *Siri Guru Granth Sahib*. Family and close friends wishing to stand behind the *Siri Guru Granth Sahib* to offer support to the couple may do so at the time indicated by the minister.

Are there any parts of the ceremony in which a guest who is not a Sikh should *not* participate?

No.

If not disruptive to the ceremony, is it okay to:

◗ **Take pictures?** Yes, but only if intended solely for personal use.
◗ **Use a flash?** Yes, but only if intended solely for personal use.
◗ **Use a video camera?** Yes, but only if intended solely for personal use.
◗ **Use a tape recorder?** Yes, but only if intended solely for personal use.

Will contributions to the *gurdwara* be collected at the ceremony?

Money or flowers may be offered to the *Siri Guru Granth Sahib* if one chooses to bow to it, which is optional. Money may be placed in a box with a slot on it or on an offering plate. Either will be in front of the *Siri Guru Granth Sahib*. Other gifts may be placed in front of the *Siri Guru Granth Sahib*.

How much is customary to contribute?

The customary contribution is $1 to $5.

AFTER THE CEREMONY

Is there usually a reception after the ceremony?

Langar, or sacred food, may be served after (and sometimes during) the ceremony. *Langar* may be served inside or outside the *gurdwara* or in a special hall built for the purpose. An additional reception at another location may take place after the *langar* where a vegetarian meal is provided. This often consists of East Indian cuisine. Since alcoholic beverages are prohibited to Sikhs, they will not be served. It is not considered impolite to decline the offered food for any reason. The reception may last anywhere from half an hour to several hours.

Would it be considered impolite to neither eat nor drink?

No.

Is there a grace or benediction before eating or drinking?

No.

Is there a grace or benediction after eating or drinking?

No.

Is there a traditional greeting for the family?

Just offer your congratulations.

Is there a traditional form of address for clergy who may be at the reception?

"*Granthi*" and then their first name, or "*Giani Ji.*"

Is it okay to leave early?

Yes.

35

Unitarian Universalist

(also known as Unitarian or Universalist)

HISTORY AND BELIEFS

The Unitarian Universalist Association was created in 1961 when the American Unitarian Association and the Universalist Church of America merged. The purpose of the union was "to cherish and spread the universal truths taught by the great prophets and teachers of humanity in every age and tradition, immemorially summarized in the Judeo-Christian heritage as love to God and love to man."

The newly-formed Unitarian Universalist Association included both American and Canadian congregations. In the same year, 1961, the Canadian Unitarian Council was organized to provide services to Canadian congregations, which are members of both bodies.

Like its predecessors, the new denomination is committed to living in the tension between humanistic liberalism and Christianity, and prefers following reason, conscience and experience to following creeds. Unitarian Universalist churches make no official pronouncements on God, the Bible, Jesus, immortality or other theological questions that are often answered with finality by more traditional religions. Instead, Unitarian Universalism deems a religious way of life as being too important to be left to rigid creeds and dogmas, and there is frequent discussion among members and clergy about whether the faith has, indeed, grown beyond Judeo-Christianity and become something more universal. Unitarian Universalists reject the attitude that salvation is attainable only through the mediation of Jesus Christ and membership in a Christian Church. Thus, many believe that Unitarian

Universalism is not a Christian faith today, although its historical and theological roots are undeniably Christian.

Unitarians trace their origins to a movement that began shortly after the death of Jesus Christ. According to present Unitarian teachings, many who personally knew Jesus rejected claims of his divinity. Instead, they focused on his humanity and his teachings, not on his alleged godliness. The movement was eventually named Arianism, after Arius, a priest from Alexandria who preached this belief. After the Council of Nicea adopted in 325 A.D. the concept of the Trinity—God, the Father; God, the Son; God, the Holy Ghost—those who embraced this idea denounced believers in God's unity as heretics.

Nevertheless, by the 16th century, Unitarian ideas had gained a foothold in Switzerland, Britain, Hungary and Italy. In 1683, the first Unitarian church to use that name was established in Transylvania. And by the first decade of the 19th century, 20 Unitarian churches had been established in England.

In the United States, Unitarianism got its impetus from the preaching and writings of William Ellery Channing in the early 19th century. Strongly concerned with liberal social causes, such as abolitionism and educational reform, the faith also gave birth to the Transcendentalism associated with Ralph Waldo Emerson and Henry David Thoreau.

While Unitarianism most often attracted the highly educated and intellectual, especially in New England, Universalism was initially an evangelistic, working-class movement with an uneducated clergy. Their "universalism" rested on a belief that all souls would eventually attain salvation. As with Unitarianism, it dates from the early days of Christianity, most notably the writings of Origen, an early Church father.

In the United States, circuit-rider ministers helped spread the faith so well that by the 1850s there were about 800,000 Universalists. By the 1900s, Universalism was the sixth largest denomination in the United States. After that, membership steadily declined, although its theological development eventually so paralleled that of Unitarianism that the two denominations could eventually merge.

In 19th-century Canada, Unitarian congregations were established in Montreal and Toronto, with the assistance of British Unitarians. Universalism entered Canada from the United States, and was largely centered in the Maritimes and Southern Ontario. Many Icelandic Lutherans in Manitoba were attracted to the more liberal Unitarian faith and established a number of congregations there. Unitarianism in Canada remained a very small faith group until the end of World War II, when there was a strong movement away from more traditional faiths, and new congregations and lay-led fellowships were established in many parts of the country.

Each local Unitarian Universalist congregation, which may be called a church, society or fellowship, adopts its own bylaws, elects its own officers and approves its budget. Each local congregation is affiliated with one of the 23 districts of the Unitarian Universalist Association of Congregations.

U.S. churches: 1,033
U.S. membership: 213,342
(1999 data from the Unitarian Universalist Association of Congregations)

Canadian churches: 44
Canadian membership: 5,038
(data from the Canadian Unitarian Council)

MARRIAGE CEREMONY

In Unitarian Universalism, marriage is the committed joining of two lives as witnessed by the community. Unitarian Universalism does not necessarily consider marriage to be a union that will last for the entirety of one's life. It also supports same-sex marriages, a stance that reflects the faith's long-time call for lesbians and gays to be fully included in the religious community and in society at large.

The wedding ceremony is a ceremony in itself. It may last about 30 to 60 minutes.

BEFORE THE CEREMONY

Are guests usually invited by a formal invitation?
Yes.

If not stated explicitly, should one assume that children are invited?
No.

If one can't attend, what should one do?
Send a written RSVP and a gift.

APPROPRIATE ATTIRE

Men: A jacket and tie. No head covering is required.

Women: A dress. Hems need not reach below the knees nor must clothing cover the arms. Open-toed shoes and modest jewelry are permissible. No head covering is required.

There are no rules regarding colors of clothing.

GIFTS

Is a gift customarily expected?

Yes. Small household items such as sheets, small appliances or kitchenware or cash in the amount of $25 to $100 are appropriate.

Should gifts be brought to the ceremony?

Gifts may be sent to the home of the newlyweds.

THE CEREMONY

Where will the ceremony take place?

In the main sanctuary of the church, in a special area elsewhere in the church or in a home.

When should guests arrive and where should they sit?

Arrive shortly before the time for which the ceremony has been called. Ushers will advise guests where to sit. Often, relatives and friends of the bride and of the groom sit on different sides of the aisle.

If arriving late, are there times when a guest should *not* enter the ceremony?

Do not enter during the processional of the wedding party.

Are there times when a guest should *not* leave the ceremony?

Do not leave during the recessional of the wedding party.

Who are the major officiants, leaders or participants at the ceremony and what do they do?

- *The minister,* who officiates at the ceremony and witnesses the vows of the bride and groom.
- *The bride and groom and members of their wedding party.*
- *Friends of the bride and groom,* who may lead those present in a meditation or read aloud a text chosen by the couple.

What books are used?

A hymnal, *Singing the Living Tradition*, edited by the Hymnbook Resource Commission (Boston, Ma.: The Unitarian Universalist Association, 1993).

To indicate the order of the ceremony:

A program may be distributed.

Will a guest who is not a Unitarian Universalist be expected to do anything other than sit?

No.

Are there any parts of the ceremony in which a guest who is not a Unitarian Universalist should *not* participate?

Yes. Do not participate in the affirmation or the welcoming of the couple from members of the congregation.

If not disruptive to the ceremony, is it okay to:
- **Take pictures?** No.
- **Use a flash?** No.
- **Use a video camera?** No.
- **Use a tape recorder?** Yes.

Will contributions to the church be collected at the ceremony?

No.

AFTER THE CEREMONY

Is there usually a reception after the ceremony?

A reception is usually held in the church reception hall, in a catering hall or at a home. Food served may be hors d'oeuvres, a complete meal, coffee, cake and alcoholic beverages. There will probably be music and dancing. The reception may last for two hours.

Would it be considered impolite to neither eat nor drink?

Yes.

Is there a grace or benediction before eating or drinking?

Yes.

Is there a grace or benediction after eating or drinking?

Sometimes.

Is there a traditional greeting for the family?

Just offer your congratulations.

Is there a traditional form of address for clergy who may be at the reception?

"Mr.," "Ms.," "Dr.," "Reverend" or simply call the clergyperson by his or her first name.

Is it okay to leave early?

Yes, but after the wedding cake has been cut and served.

36

United Church of Canada

HISTORY AND BELIEFS

The United Church of Canada was created by an Act of Parliament in 1925 as a union of the country's Presbyterian, Methodist and Congregational denominations. In Western Canada, in communities unable to afford the luxury of separate churches, a number of informal Union churches had already formed, applying pressure on parent denominations to amalgamate.

Although Presbyterians provided the initial push for the three-denomination Union, in the end they also offered its greatest opposition; approximately one-third of Presbyterian congregations voted not to unite. The Methodist and Congregational denominations entered the Church Union as a whole.

The United Church sees itself as having a mandate to work toward further unions. In 1968, it was joined by the Evangelical United Brethren. A proposed union with the Anglican Church of Canada, however, foundered in the 1970s.

Its worship and policies are, inevitably, a product of its founding traditions. From the Methodists, the United Church inherited a passion for social justice; from the Presbyterians, a conciliar system for internal governance; from the Congregationalists, a stubborn refusal to be bound by arbitrary doctrine or dogma.

The United Church has been at the forefront of social change in Canada. It was the first mainline denomination in the world to ordain women as ministers. It welcomed draft resisters during the Vietnam War, lobbied against alcohol and tobacco, urged recognition of the Republic of China, endorsed women's right to choice of abortion and, most recently, ruled that homosexuality is not, in and of itself, a bar to ordination.

187

The national court of the United Church is the General Council, which meets every three years. Only the General Council speaks for the United Church. Between Councils, elected officials of the church or various committees or divisions may interpret or comment on the Council's policies. Surprisingly, there are few doctrinal statements. The *Basis of Union* of 1925 contains *Twenty Articles of Faith*, developed as a statement of the common faith of the three founding denominations. The only *Statement of Faith* issued by the United Church itself came in 1940, with a teaching *Catechism* in 1942. In 1968, the General Council authorized a "New Creed" as an authentic expression of the United Church's faith. This "Creed" has since been revised twice, to eliminate exclusively masculine language, and to add concern for the natural environment.

The Congregationalist openness to diverse viewpoints means that ministers are required only to be in "essential agreement" with the *Twenty Articles*. As a result, the church's ministry encompasses a wide variety of theological viewpoints.

As a national denomination, the United Church has no branches or subsidiaries in any other country. It does have working partnerships with a number of other churches in other parts of the world. The United Church maintains membership in the world associations to which its predecessors belonged, such as the World Alliance of Reformed Churches.

Canadian churches: 3,872
Canadian membership: 720,000
(*data from* The United Church of Canada Yearbook *and the*
1998 Yearbook of American and Canadian Churches)

MARRIAGE CEREMONY

In the United Church, marriage is the formal ceremony in which a couple make lifetime vows of commitment to each other, in the presence of God and of their families and friends.

The ceremony is rarely combined with a regular worship service. It is both a civil and a religious ceremony, and may last anywhere from 15 minutes to an hour, depending on the number of musical numbers performed, the length of the minister's address to the couple and the time required for signing the official register.

BEFORE THE CEREMONY

Are guests usually invited by a formal invitation?
Yes. Anyone may attend the religious ceremony of marriage, without requiring an invitation. But an invitation is required for the reception that follows the wedding ceremony.

If not stated explicitly, should one assume children are invited?
No.

If one cannot attend, what should one do?
Reply with regrets, and send a gift.

APPROPRIATE ATTIRE

Men: Generally, a suit or jacket and tie.

Women: A dress or pants suit. Clothing and jewelry should be relatively modest.

Dress for both men and women depends more on the local culture than on religious standards. The more elaborate the wedding ceremony, the more formal attire should be. There are no religious rules applicable to attire at wedding ceremonies.

GIFTS

Is a gift ordinarily expected?
Yes, if you have received a formal invitation. If you are simply attending a public ceremony, a gift would be appreciated, but is not necessary. Items suitable for helping the couple set up their home—small appliances, bedding, sheets, towels and other household gifts—are appropriate.

Should gifts be brought to the ceremony?
No. Gifts should be sent to the home of the newlyweds.

THE CEREMONY

Where will the ceremony take place?
Normally, in the sanctuary, the place of worship. However, United Church clergy have shown themselves remarkably adaptable, and may be willing to perform the ceremony outside the church—for example, in a garden or on a beach.

If the ceremony is held in a church, the actual ceremony will take place in front of the congregation, immediately before the chancel.

When should guests arrive and where should they sit?
Arrive early. In most weddings, ushers will show guests where to sit. It is still traditional, in many places, to have friends of the groom sit on one side of the sanctuary, and friends of the bride on the other side.

If arriving late, are there times when a guest should *not* enter the ceremony?

Ushers will assist latecomers.

Are there times when a guest should *not* leave the ceremony?

It is considered poor taste to leave before the ceremony is completed.

Who are the major officiants, leaders or participants at the ceremony and what do they do?

- *The minister(s),* who leads the service.
- *The couple,* who exchange vows.
- *The wedding party,* who provide support and witness the vows.

What books are used?

Most likely the congregation's normal hymnbook(s). Often the hymns and other responses are printed out in a special program or bulletin.

To indicate the order of the ceremony:

Usually a printed program or bulletin will be provided, supplemented by announcements from the minister.

Will a guest who is not a member of the United Church be expected to do anything other than sit?

Guests are invited to participate in all aspects of a marriage ceremony that do not violate their own personal beliefs.

If not disruptive to the service, is it okay to:

- **Take pictures?** Possibly. But ask first.
- **Use a flash?** No, unless you have received permission.
- **Use a video camera?** Possibly. Ask first.
- **Use a tape recorder?** Probably.

Will contributions to the church be collected at the ceremony?

No.

AFTER THE CEREMONY

Is there usually a reception after the ceremony?

Yes. Sometimes it is held in a hall or room adjacent to the church sanctuary. More commonly, it is catered in an entirely separate location. Food and beverages may be served; there may be dancing or other activities. Alcoholic beverages may be served, if the reception is not on church premises. The reception may last anywhere from an hour to most of a night.

Would it be considered impolite to neither eat nor drink?
No. Guests should feel free to apply their own dietary standards.

Is there a grace or benediction before eating or drinking?
Sometimes. It depends on the family's preferences.

Is there a grace or benediction after eating or drinking?
No.

Is there a traditional greeting for the family?
No.

Is there a traditional form of address for clergy who may be at the reception?
Formally, clergy should be addressed as "Mr.," "Mrs." or "Ms.," followed by their last name. It is impolite to refer to them simply as "Reverend." Informally, many prefer to be addressed by their first names.

Is it okay to leave early?
Yes, but it's usually expected that you will stay until at least the toasts have been made and the wedding cake served.

37

United Church of Christ

HISTORY AND BELIEFS

Formed in 1957 by the merger of two churches, the United Church of Christ is one of the newer Protestant denominations in the United States.

The merger was between the Congregational Christian Churches, whose roots date back to 16th century England and to the Puritan and Separatist movements that settled New England; and the Evangelical and Reform Church, which had previously been formed by combining the German Reformed Church and the Evangelical Synod of North America.

According to the constitution of the United Church of Christ, Jesus Christ is the "sole Head" of the Church and each local congregation is its "basic unit." Local churches choose their own pastors and determine policy regarding membership, worship, budget and programs. Congregations cooperate in area groupings called "associations" and in larger regional bodies called "conferences." The General Synod, the Church's central deliberative body, meets biennially to conduct denominational business. More than half the Church's membership is in the New England and Midwestern states.

U.S. churches: 6,110
U.S. membership: 1.5 million
(*data from the* 1998 Yearbook of American and Canadian Churches)

MARRIAGE CEREMONY

The United Church of Christ teaches that the essence of marriage is a covenanted commitment that has its foundation in the faithfulness of

God's love. The marriage ceremony is the occasion on which two people unite as husband and wife in the mutual exchange of covenant promises. The presiding official represents the Church and gives the marriage the Church's blessing. The congregation joins in affirming the marriage and in offering support and thanksgiving for the new family.

Usually, the wedding is a ceremony in itself. Only rarely is it part of a regular Sunday worship service. It may last 30 minutes to one hour.

BEFORE THE CEREMONY

Are guests usually invited by a formal invitation?
Yes.

If not stated explicitly, should one assume that children are invited?
No.

If one can't attend, what should one do?
RSVP with regrets and send a gift.

APPROPRIATE ATTIRE

Men: A jacket and tie. No head covering is required.

Women: A dress or a skirt and blouse. Clothing need not cover the arms and hems need not reach below the knees. Open-toed shoes and modest jewelry are permissible. No head covering is required.

There are no rules regarding colors of clothing.

GIFTS

Is a gift customarily expected?
Yes. Cash or bonds or household items (such as sheets, kitchenware or small appliances) are appropriate.

Should gifts be brought to the ceremony?
Bring gifts to the reception that follows the wedding ceremony.

THE CEREMONY

Where will the ceremony take place?
In the church's main sanctuary or a special room in the church, or in a home, a catering hall or outdoors.

When should guests arrive and where should they sit?
Arrive shortly before the time for which the wedding has been scheduled. Usually, ushers will advise guests where to sit.

If arriving late, are there times when a guest should *not* enter the ceremony?

Do not enter during the processional or recessional of the wedding party or during the recitation of wedding vows. Follow the ushers' guidance for entering the ceremony.

Are there times when a guest should *not* leave the ceremony?

Do not leave during the processional or recessional of the wedding party or during the recitation of wedding vows. Follow the ushers' guidance for leaving the ceremony.

Who are the major officiants, leaders or participants at the ceremony and what do they do?

- *The minister(s) or pastor(s),* who preside over the ceremony.
- *The bride and groom, other members of the wedding party.*
- *Lector(s) or reader(s),* who, at some weddings, may read the Scriptures aloud to those present.
- *Deacons,* who help serve communion, which is not served at all weddings.
- *Ushers,* who greet and seat guests at most weddings.

What books are used?

The most commonly used of several Protestant Bibles is The Holy Bible, New Revised Standard Version (New York: National Council of Churches, 1989). Also used is *The New Century Hymnal* (Cleveland, Ohio: The Pilgrim Press, 1995).

To indicate the order of the ceremony:

The minister will make periodic announcements.

Will a guest who is not a member of the United Church of Christ be expected to do anything other than sit?

Guests are expected to join congregants when they stand during the service. It is entirely optional for them to read prayers aloud and sing with the congregation. In most United Church of Christ congregations, congregants do not kneel. In those churches where kneeling occurs, it is optional for guests to join in. Those guests who do not kneel should remain seated.

Are there any parts of the ceremony in which a guest who is not a member of the United Church of Christ should *not* participate?

No.

If not disruptive to the ceremony, is it okay to:

◾ **Take pictures?** Practice varies. Ask the pastor in advance.

◾ **Use a flash?** Practice varies. Ask the pastor in advance.

◾ **Use a video camera?** Practice varies. Ask the pastor in advance.

◾ **Use a tape recorder?** Practice varies. Ask the pastor in advance.

Will contributions to the church be collected at the ceremony?
Only if the wedding is part of a regular Sunday worship service. If so, ushers will pass offering plates through the congregation during the service.

How much is customary to contribute?
If guests choose to do so, contributions between $1 and $10 are appropriate.

AFTER THE CEREMONY

Is there usually a reception after the ceremony?
Yes. It is usually in a catering hall, at a home or in a church reception hall. There is usually a reception line and a full meal is served. If the reception is not in the church, there may be alcoholic beverages and/or music and dancing. The reception may last two hours or more.

Would it be considered impolite to neither eat nor drink?
No.

Is there a grace or benediction before eating or drinking?
Grace will be said if a full meal is served.

Is there a grace or benediction after eating or drinking?
No.

Is there a traditional greeting for the family?
Just offer your congratulations.

Is there a traditional form of address for clergy who may be at the reception?
Some are addressed as "Pastor." Some prefer to be addressed as "Mr." or "Ms." or, if the church bulletin distributed at services so indicates, as "Dr." Many United Church of Christ clergy prefer being addressed by their first name.

Is it okay to leave early?
Yes.

38

Wesleyan

HISTORY AND BELIEFS

The Wesleyan movement, which began in the early 18th century, centers around the scriptural truth concerning the doctrine and experience of holiness, which declares that the atonement of Christ for the sins of humanity provides not only for the regeneration of sinners, but also for the entire sanctification of believers. "Regeneration" is often referred to as "The New Birth." Members of the Wesleyan Church believe that when a person repents of his or her sin and believes in Jesus Christ, then that person is also adopted into the family of God and assured of his or her salvation through the witness of the Holy Spirit. "Sanctification" is considered to be the work of the Holy Spirit through which one is separated from sin and is enabled to love God. John Wesley, whose preaching began the faith in England, referred to this teaching and experience as "perfect love."

Wesley, an Anglican priest, was a prodigious evangelical preacher, writer and organizer. While a student at Oxford University, he and his brother, Charles, led the Holy Club of devout students, whom scoffers called the "Methodists."

Wesley's teachings affirmed the freedom of human will as promoted by grace. He saw each person's depth of sin matched by the height of sanctification to which the Holy Spirit, the empowering spirit of God, can lead persons of faith.

Although Wesley remained an Anglican and disavowed attempts to form a new church, the "societies" he founded eventually became another church body known as Methodism. During a conference in Baltimore,

Maryland, in 1784, the Methodist Episcopal Church was founded as an ecclesiastical organization.

John Wesley, as well as the early Methodist leaders in the United States, had uncompromisingly denounced slavery. But many ministers and members of the Methodist Episcopal Church eventually owned slaves because of the economic advantages of doing so. When some Methodist ministers in the North began to agitate for abolition, others tried to silence them. By 1843, enough churches had withdrawn from the Church to form their own denomination, which they called the Wesleyan Methodist Connection. After the Civil War, some churches in the Connection rejoined the larger Methodist body. Others were convinced that the effects of slavery had not yet been eradicated and that their stand against liquor and secret societies could best be maintained by being independent.

The church's name changed three times: In 1891, to the Wesleyan Methodist Connection (or Church) of America; in 1947, to the Wesleyan Methodist Church of America; and in 1968, to the Wesleyan Church when it merged with the Pilgrim Holiness Church. The Wesleyan Church of Canada, which consists of the Atlantic and Central districts, is the Canadian portion of the Wesleyan Church. The roots of the Central district extend back to 1889 and the former Wesleyan Methodist Church of America, while those of the Atlantic district reach back to 1888 and the Reformed Baptist Church.

Building on its abolitionist heritage, the Wesleyan Church takes strong social stands. These include opposing discrimination against interracial marriage or against age discrimination. The Church also invokes biblical principles against homosexuality and abortion, and lends moral support to any member who claims exemption from military combat as a conscientious objector and asks to serve the nation as a noncombatant.

Each local church membership convenes in a local church conference at least once a year to address the business of the local church to elect the local board of administration that is chaired by the senior pastor. Members vote for the pastor of their choice and renew this at a vote taken at intervals of approximately every four years. The pastoral contract is subject to a ratifying vote by the district conference to which the local church belongs.

A quadrennial General Conference elects three General Superintendents who serve as the Church's titular, administrative and spiritual leaders. The General Conference, which is composed of equal numbers of laypersons and clergy, also elects five ministry directors and a General Secretary who serve the denomination on a full-time basis.

U.S. churches: 1,580
U.S. membership: 118,021
(*data from the* 1998 Yearbook of American and Canadian Churches)

Canadian churches: 87
Canadian membership: 7,500
(*data from the Wesleyan Church of Canada, Central District*)

MARRIAGE CEREMONY

The Wesleyan Church teaches that man and women are both created in the image of God, and that human sexuality reflects that image in terms of intimate love, communication, fellowship, subordination of the self to the larger whole and fulfillment. The marriage relationship is a metaphor for God's relationship with His covenant people and for revealing the truth that relationship is between one God with His people. Therefore, God's plan for human sexuality is that it be expressed only in a monogamous life-long relationship between a man and a woman within the framework of marriage. This is the only relationship designed for the birth and the rearing of children.

The only biblical grounds for even considering divorce is the sexual sin of the spouse. This includes adultery, homosexuality, bestiality or incest.

The wedding ceremony is a ceremony in itself. It may last about 15 to 30 minutes.

BEFORE THE CEREMONY

Are guests usually invited by a formal invitation?
Yes.

If not stated explicitly, should one assume that children are invited?
Yes.

If one can't attend, what should one do?
RSVP with regrets and send a gift.

APPROPRIATE ATTIRE

Men: A jacket and tie. No head covering is required.

Women: A dress or a skirt and blouse. Hems need not reach below the knees nor must clothing cover the arms. Open-toed shoes and modest jewelry are permissible. No head covering is required.

There are no rules regarding colors of clothing.

GIFTS

Is a gift customarily expected?

Yes. Small household items such as sheets, small appliances or kitchen-ware or cash or bonds in the amount of $15 to $100 are appropriate.

Should gifts be brought to the ceremony?

Gifts may either be brought to the ceremony or sent to the home of the newlyweds.

THE CEREMONY

Where will the ceremony take place?

In the main auditorium of the church.

When should guests arrive and where should they sit?

Arrive shortly before the time for which the ceremony has been called. Ushers will advise guests where to sit.

If arriving late, are there times when a guest should *not* enter the ceremony?

Do not enter during the processional of the wedding party.

Are there times when a guest should *not* leave the ceremony?

Do not leave during the recessional of the wedding party.

Who are the major officiants, leaders or participants at the ceremony and what do they do?

- *The minister,* who officiates at the ceremony and witnesses the vows of the bride and groom.
- *The bride and groom and their wedding party.*

What books are used?

No books are used by guests and participants.

To indicate the order of the ceremony:

A program will be distributed.

Will a guest who is not a member of the Wesleyan Church be expected to do anything other than sit?

It is expected for each guest to stand with the other guests.

Are there any parts of the ceremony in which a guest who is not a member of the Wesleyan Church should *not* participate?

No.

If not disruptive to the ceremony, is it okay to:
- **Take pictures?** No.
- **Use a flash?** No.
- **Use a video camera?** No.
- **Use a tape recorder?** Yes.

Will contributions to the church be collected at the ceremony?

No.

AFTER THE CEREMONY

Is there usually a reception after the ceremony?

A reception is held in the church reception hall, in a catering hall or at a home. Food served may be hors d'oeuvres, finger foods, punch, coffee and cake. There will be no alcoholic beverages. There may be music, especially classical, contemporary or religious, but no dancing. The reception may last for one and a half to two hours.

Would it be considered impolite to neither eat nor drink?

No.

Is there a grace or benediction before eating or drinking?

Yes.

Is there a grace or benediction after eating or drinking?

No.

Is there a traditional greeting for the family?

Just offer your congratulations.

Is there a traditional form of address for clergy who may be at the reception?

"Pastor."

Is it okay to leave early?

Yes.

About SKYLIGHT PATHS Publishing

SkyLight Paths Publishing is creating a place where people of different spiritual traditions come together for challenge and inspiration, a place where we can help each other understand the mystery that lies at the heart of our existence.

Through spirituality, our religious beliefs are increasingly becoming a part of our lives—rather than apart from our lives. While many of us may be more interested than ever in spiritual growth, we may be less firmly planted in traditional religion. Yet, we do want to deepen our relationship to the sacred, to learn from our own as well as from other faith traditions, and to practice in new ways.

SkyLight Paths sees both believers and seekers as a community that increasingly transcends traditional boundaries of religion and denomination. Many people want to learn from each other, *walking together, finding the way.*

We at SkyLight Paths take great care to produce beautiful books that present meaningful spiritual content in a form that reflects the art of making high quality books. Therefore, we want to acknowledge those who contributed to the production of this book.

PRODUCTION
Marian B. Wallace & Bridgett Taylor

EDITORIAL
David O'Neal, Amanda Dupuis, Emily Wichland,
Martha McKinney & Sandra Korinchak

COVER DESIGN & TYPESETTING
Drena Fagen, New York, New York

TEXT DESIGN
Chelsea Cloeter, Chelsea Designs, Scotia, New York

TYPESETTING
Douglas S. Porter, Desktop Services & Publishing, San Antonio, Texas

COVER & TEXT PRINTING AND BINDING
Versa Press, East Peoria, Illinois

Other Interesting Books—Spirituality

Show Me Your Way
The Complete Guide to Exploring Interfaith Spiritual Direction
by *Howard A. Addison*

The rediscovery of an ancient spiritual practice— reimagined for the modern seeker.

This revealing book introduces people of all faiths—even those with no particular religious involvement—to the concept and practice of spiritual direction and, for the first time, to the dynamics of *interfaith* spiritual direction. Explores how spiritual direction differs within each major religious tradition, and how and where to find guidance within your faith community or beyond it. You really can gain spiritual inspiration from other faiths—*without leaving your own.* 5½ x 8½, 208 pp, HC, ISBN 1-893361-12-8 **$21.95**

Waking Up: *A Week Inside a Zen Monastery*
by *Jack Maguire;* Foreword by *John Daido Loori, Roshi*

An essential guide to what it's like to spend a week inside a Zen Buddhist monastery.

The notion of spending days at a time in silence and meditation amid the serene beauty of a Zen monastery may be appealing—but how do you do it, and what can you really expect from the experience? This essential guide provides the answers for everyone who's just curious, as well as for those who have dreamed of actually giving it a try and want to know where to begin. 6 x 9, 208 pp, b/w photographs, HC, ISBN 1-893361-13-6 **$21.95**

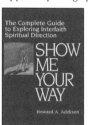

The New Millennium Spiritual Journey
Change Your Life—Develop Your Spiritual Priorities with Help from Today's Most Inspiring Spiritual Teachers
Created by *the Editors at SkyLight Paths*

A life-changing resource for reimagining your spiritual life.

Set your own course of reflection and spiritual transformation with the help of self-tests, spirituality exercises, sacred texts from many traditions, time capsule pages, and helpful suggestions from more than 20 spiritual teachers. 7 x 9, 144 pp, Quality PB Original, ISBN 1-893361-05-5 **$16.95**

Or phone, fax or mail to: SKYLIGHT PATHS Publishing

Sunset Farm Offices, Route 4 • P.O. Box 237 • Woodstock, Vermont 05091
Tel: (802) 457-4000   Fax: (802) 457-4004   www.skylightpaths.com
Credit card orders (800) 962-4544 (9AM–5PM ET Monday–Friday)

Generous discounts on quantity orders. Satisfaction guaranteed. Prices subject to change.

Spirituality

Who Is My God?
An Innovative Guide to Finding Your Spiritual Identity
Created by *the Editors at SkyLight Paths*

Spiritual Type™ + Tradition Indicator = Spiritual Identity

Your Spiritual Identity is an undeniable part of who you are—whether you've thought much about it or not. This dynamic resource provides a helpful framework to begin or deepen your spiritual growth. Start by taking the unique Spiritual Identity Self-Test™; tabulate your results; then explore one, two or more of twenty-eight faiths/spiritual paths followed in America today. "An innovative and entertaining way to think—and rethink—about your own spiritual path, or perhaps even to find one." —Dan Wakefield, author of *How Do We Know When It's God?* 6 x 9, 160 pp, Quality PB Original, ISBN 1-893361-08-X **$15.95**

Spiritual Manifestos: *Visions for Renewed Religious Life in America from Young Spiritual Leaders of Many Faiths*
Edited by *Niles Elliot Goldstein*; Preface by *Martin E. Marty*

Discover the reasons why so many people have kept organized religion at arm's length.

Here, ten young spiritual leaders, most in their mid-thirties, who span the spectrum of religious traditions—Protestant, Catholic, Jewish, Buddhist, Unitarian Universalist—present the innovative ways they are transforming our spiritual communities and our lives. "These ten articulate young spiritual leaders engender hope for the vitality of 21st-century religion." —Forrest Church, Minister of All Souls Church in New York City
6 x 9, 256 pp, HC, ISBN 1-893361-09-8 **$21.95**

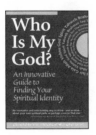  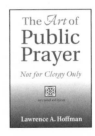

The Art of Public Prayer: *Not for Clergy Only*
by *Lawrence A. Hoffman*

A resource for worshipers today looking to change hardened worship patterns that stand in the way of everyday spirituality.

Written for laypeople and clergy of any denomination, this ecumenical introduction to meaningful public prayer is for everyone who cares about religion today.
6 x 9, 288 pp, Quality PB, ISBN 1-893361-06-3 **$17.95**

Spirituality

A Heart of Stillness
A Complete Guide to Learning the Art of Meditation
by *David A. Cooper*

The only complete, nonsectarian guide to meditation, from one of our most respected spiritual teachers.

Experience what mystics have experienced for thousands of years. *A Heart of Stillness* helps you acquire on your own, with minimal guidance, the skills of various styles of meditation. Draws upon the wisdom teachings of Christianity, Judaism, Buddhism, Hinduism, and Islam as it teaches you the processes of purification, concentration, and mastery in detail.
5½ x 8½, 272 pp, Quality PB, ISBN 1-893361-03-9 **$16.95**

Silence, Simplicity & Solitude
A Complete Guide to Spiritual Retreat at Home
by *David A. Cooper*

The classic personal spiritual retreat guide that enables readers to create their own self-guided spiritual retreat at home.

Award-winning author David Cooper traces personal mystical retreat in all of the world's major traditions, describing the varieties of spiritual practices for modern spiritual seekers. Cooper shares the techniques and practices that encompass the personal spiritual retreat experience, allowing readers to enhance their meditation practices and create an effective, self-guided spiritual retreat in their own homes—without the instruction of a meditation teacher. 5½ x 8½, 336 pp, Quality PB, ISBN 1-893361-04-7 **$16.95**

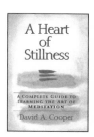 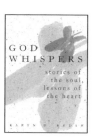   

God Whispers: *Stories of the Soul, Lessons of the Heart*
by Rabbi Karyn D. Kedar 6 x 9, 176 pp, Quality PB, ISBN 1-58023-088-1 **$15.95**;
HC, ISBN 1-58023-023-7 **$19.95**

The Empty Chair: *Finding Hope and Joy—*
Timeless Wisdom from a Hasidic Master, Rebbe Nachman of Breslov **AWARD WINNER!**
Adapted by Moshe Mykoff and the Breslov Research Institute
4 x 6, 128 pp, Deluxe PB, 2-color text, ISBN 1-879045-67-2 **$9.95**

The Gentle Weapon: *Prayers for Everyday and Not-So-Everyday Moments*
Adapted from the Wisdom of Rebbe Nachman of Breslov by Moshe Mykoff and
S. C. Mizrahi, with the Breslov Research Institute
4 x 6, 144 pp, Deluxe PB, 2-color text, ISBN 1-58023-022-9 **$9.95**

Children's Spirituality

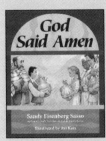

God Said Amen

For ages 4 & up

by *Sandy Eisenberg Sasso*
Full-color illus. by *Avi Katz*

MULTICULTURAL, NONDENOMINATIONAL, NONSECTARIAN

A warm and inspiring tale of two kingdoms: Midnight Kingdom is overflowing with water but has no oil to light its lamps; Desert Kingdom is blessed with oil but has no water to grow its gardens. The kingdoms' rulers ask God for help but are too stubborn to ask each other. It takes a minstrel, a pair of royal riding-birds and their young keepers, and a simple act of kindness to show that they need only reach out to each other to find the answers to their prayers.

9 x 12, 32 pp, HC, Full-color illus., ISBN 1-58023-080-6 **$16.95**

For Heaven's Sake

For ages 4 & up

by *Sandy Eisenberg Sasso*; Full-color illus. by *Kathryn Kunz Finney*

Everyone talked about heaven: "Thank heavens." "Heaven forbid." "For heaven's sake, Isaiah." But no one would say what heaven was or how to find it. So Isaiah decides to find out, by seeking answers from many different people. "This book is a reminder of how well Sandy Sasso knows the minds of children. But it may surprise—and delight—readers to find how well she knows us grown-ups too." —*Maria Harris*, National Consultant in Religious Education, and author of *Teaching and Religious Imagination*
9 x 12, 32 pp, HC, Full-color illus., ISBN 1-58023-054-7 **$16.95**

But God Remembered:

For ages 8 & up

Stories of Women from Creation to the Promised Land
by *Sandy Eisenberg Sasso*; Full-color illus. by *Bethanne Andersen*

A fascinating collection of four different stories of women only briefly mentioned in biblical tradition and religious texts. Award-winning author Sasso vibrantly brings to life courageous and strong women from ancient tradition; all teach important values through their actions and faith. "Exquisite. . . . A book of beauty, strength and spirituality." —*Association of Bible Teachers* 9 x 12, 32 pp, HC, Full-color illus., ISBN 1-879045-43-5 **$16.95**

God in Between

For ages 4 & up

by *Sandy Eisenberg Sasso*; Full-color illus. by *Sally Sweetland*

If you wanted to find God, where would you look? A magical, mythical tale that teaches that God can be found where we are: within all of us and the relationships between us. "This happy and wondrous book takes our children on a sweet and holy journey into God's presence." —*Rabbi Wayne Dosick, Ph.D.*, author of *Golden Rules* and *Soul Judaism*
9 x 12, 32 pp, HC, Full-color illus., ISBN 1-879045-86-9 **$16.95**

Children's Spirituality

In Our Image
God's First Creatures

For ages
4 & up

by *Nancy Sohn Swartz*

Full-color illus. by *Melanie Hall*

A playful new twist on the Creation story—from the perspective of the animals. Celebrates the interconnectedness of nature and the harmony of all living things. "The vibrantly colored illustrations nearly leap off the page in this delightful interpretation." —School Library Journal

•AWARD WINNER•

"A message all children should hear, presented in words and pictures that children will find irresistible." —*Rabbi Harold Kushner*, author of *When Bad Things Happen to Good People*

9 x 12, 32 pp, HC, Full-color illus., ISBN 1-879045-99-0 **$16.95**

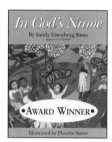

God's Paintbrush

For ages
4 & up

by *Sandy Eisenberg Sasso*; Full-color illus. by *Annette Compton*

Invites children of all faiths and backgrounds to encounter God openly in their own lives. Wonderfully interactive; provides questions adult and child can explore together at the end of each episode. "An excellent way to honor the imaginative breadth and depth of the spiritual life of the young." —*Dr. Robert Coles*, Harvard University

11 x 8½, 32 pp, HC, Full-color illus., ISBN 1-879045-22-2 **$16.95**

Also available: **A Teacher's Guide**
8½ x 11, 32 pp, PB, ISBN 1-879045-57-5 **$6.95**

God's Paintbrush Celebration Kit 9½ x 12, HC, Includes 5 sessions/40 full-color Activity Sheets and Teacher Folder with complete instructions, ISBN 1-58023-050-4 **$21.95**

In God's Name

For ages
4 & up

by *Sandy Eisenberg Sasso*; Full-color illus. by *Phoebe Stone*

Like an ancient myth in its poetic text and vibrant illustrations, this award-winning modern fable about the search for God's name celebrates the diversity and, at the same time, the unity of all the people of the world. "What a lovely, healing book!" —*Madeleine L'Engle*

9 x 12, 32 pp, HC, Full-color illus., ISBN 1-879045-26-5 **$16.95**

Children's Spirituality

Becoming Me: *A Story of Creation*
by *Martin Boroson*
Full-color illus. by *Christopher Gilvan-Cartwright*

For ages 4 & up

NONDENOMINATIONAL, NONSECTARIAN

Told in the personal "voice" of the Creator, here is a story about creation and relationship that is about each one of us. In simple words and with radiant illustrations, the Creator tells an intimate story about love, about friendship and playing, about our world—and about ourselves. And with each turn of the page, we're reminded that we just might be closer to our Creator than we think!

8 x 10, 32 pp, Full-color illus., HC, ISBN 1-893361-11-X **$16.95**

A Prayer for the Earth
The Story of Naamah, Noah's Wife
by *Sandy Eisenberg Sasso*
Full-color illus. by *Bethanne Andersen*

For ages 4 & up

NONDENOMINATIONAL, NONSECTARIAN

This new story, based on an ancient text, opens readers' religious imaginations to new ideas about the well-known story of the Flood. When God tells Noah to bring the animals of the world onto the ark, God also calls on Naamah, Noah's wife, to save each plant on Earth. "A lovely tale. . . . Children of all ages should be drawn to this parable for our times."
—*Tomie de Paola*, artist/author of books for children
9 x 12, 32 pp, HC, Full-color illus., ISBN 1-879045-60-5 **$16.95**

The 11th Commandment
Wisdom from Our Children
by The Children of America

For all ages

MULTICULTURAL, NONDENOMINATIONAL, NONSECTARIAN

"If there were an Eleventh Commandment, what would it be?" Children of many religious denominations across America answer this question—in their own drawings and words. "A rare book of spiritual celebration for all people, of all ages, for all time."—Bookviews
8 x 10, 48 pp. HC, Full-color illus., ISBN 1-879045-46-X **$16.95**

What Is God's Name? (A Board Book)
An abridged board book version of the award-winning *In God's Name*.

For ages 0–4

5 x 5, 24 pp, Board, Full-color illus., ISBN 1-893361-10-1 **$7.95**

  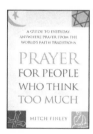